THE FARMER BOY'S ~~TAIL~~ TALE

From the Farm to Bank Vice President

WALT HEAPS

Copyright © 2023 Walt Heaps
All Rights Reserved

Year of the Book
135 Glen Avenue
Glen Rock, PA 17327

ISBN: 978-1-64649-307-4 (print)
ISBN: 978-1-64649-308-1 (ebook)

This book is a memoir. It reflects the author's present recollections of experiences over time.

This book or any portion thereof may not be reproduced or used in any manner whatsoever without the express written permission of the author, except for the use of brief quotations in a book review.

Printed in the United States of America

Contents

1 Heaps & Carico 1
2 Walter Arly Heaps 5
3 75-Acre Farm... Our Homeplace 15
4 The Murder of Harold D. Dinsmore 31
5 The Funeral and Trial.. 37
6 Life Moves On 47
7 Meeting Kathy 49
8 Making a Home.. 55
9 New House, New Job, New Child 63
10 Strange Occasions 69
11 Westward Bound... 71
12 Bank Bound 83
13 Bank Shenanigans 89
14 Kids, etc. 93
15 School Board 97
16 Russian Exchange Teacher................................... 99
17 Our Trip to Russia 105
18 Alaska via Las Vegas?... 115
19 Australia Bound.. 123
20 Y2K Scare 129
21 Panama Canal: Our Last Adventure 131
22 End of an Era 137

Dedicated to all my grandchildren

HEAPS & CARICO

My father, Walter Richardson Heaps, was born on April 2, 1922, the sixth son of Charles and Ozella Heaps. That same year, the Lincoln Memorial was dedicated by President William Howard Taft, "My Man" by Fanny Brice was #1 in the Pop charts, and Prohibition continued—a nationwide ban on the production, importation, transportation, and sale of alcohol—which made even home-brewing illegal.

Back then, at age 18, all boys were required to report to the closest recuitment office and sign up for the draft. It was like a lottery where you were assigned a number, and when your number came up, you had to report for duty.

My mother, Arlene Athlyn Carico, was born on November 27, 1923, just a few months after the "Hollywoodland" sign was erected in the hills above Los Angeles. She was the fourth and youngest child of Walter M. Carico (1892–1974) and Ethel Gentry Carico.

Mom played on the girls basketball team and graduated, while Dad never finished high school. He worked as a farmer and contractor, and Mom worked for the Southeastern School District for 21 years.

They were married on December 15, 1940. The two of them enjoyed Country music. Dad wrote his signature song, "Blue Eyes," though he never recorded it because that would cost a lot of money.

Recently my brother Scott said he found the song lyrics, but I have not heard him sing it yet. I am looking forward to hearing it in the near future.

I remember Dad and Mom singing "Blue Eyes" at picnics and Sunset Park, where bluegrass and Nashville-style music concerts were held each Sunday from spring to fall. The nearby New River Ranch, near Rising Sun, Maryland, also held such concerts. All the big names came to Sunset Park, including Roy Acuff, Ernest Tubb, Patsy Cline, George Jones, and Johnny Cash.

Dad holding me and my brother Dale. I'm wearing the hat I used to ask for donations when Dad performed.

Dad once opened a show for Porter Wagoner and Norma Jean, known back then as "Pretty Norma Jean," who at that time was the prettiest girl I had seen. She even let me sit on her lap. Looking back she might have been the prettiest girl ever.

When I was very young, sometimes I would sit on Dad's knee and hold out a cowboy hat for monetary donations after performances. When Mom and Dad played and sang together, it somehow made us feel proud and gave me a sense of belonging to a family.

Dad died on December 22, 1989.

Mom died on April 15, 2010.

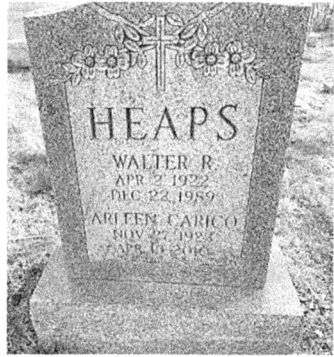

The Heaps Family Crest

The surname Heap, spelled sometimes as Heaps, was first found in Lancashire where they held a family seat and were granted lands by Duke William of Normandy, their liege Lord, for distinguished assistance at the Battle of Hastings in 1066 A.D.

WALTER ARLY HEAPS

I was born November 18, 1941, the first of nine children. I was not good-looking, but not humdrum either.

I have been told the first time I went out of the house was to visit my aunt, Helen, on December 7, 1941. That same day, Japan launched a surprise attack on Pearl Harbor, and President Roosevelt subsequently declared war. I am sure it was just a coincidence, but it kind of reflects how the rest of my life went.

Three days later, Germany and Italy joined their ally Japan by declaring war against the United States, and our country officially entered World War II.

Polio was becoming a crisis. It paralyzed many children, though no one in our immediate family contracted it, which was a blessing.

Still, some extended family members were affected, but luckily it was not fatal for them.

My first home.

I was three years old when Dad was called to active military duty in April 1944. He didn't enlist. His number just came up and he was drafted. It didn't matter that he was the sole income earner or that he had two children.

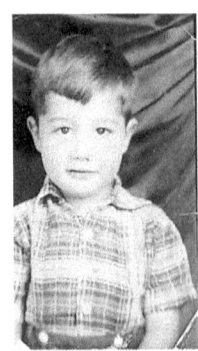

The average cost of a new home then was $3,450, while the average annual income was $2,400. Bing Crosby crooned, "Swinging on a Star," and *Casablanca* was named Outstanding Motion Picture at the Academy Awards.

Dad was stationed in Korea, and this was not an easy time for my mother, who had two small boys to look after.

During World War II, every American was issued a series of ration books which had removable stamps that were good for items like sugar, meat, cooking oil, canned goods, and even gasoline. This was meant to ensure fair distributions of food and other commodities. You couldn't buy any rationed items without giving the grocer the right ration stamp.

Mom also collected S&H green stamps, which was a kind of rewards program. These trading stamps could be taken to a redemption center and traded for all kinds of items. My mother did what she had to do to make life easier for the whole family.

During this time and earlier, many of the feed suppliers came out with flowered feed sacks. My mother and others used these sacks when empty to make aprons and various articles of clothing for our family.

An example of a feed sack dress.

A Pillsbury Flour manager was quoted in 1946 in *Time* magazine: "They used to say that when the wind blew across the south, you could see our trademark on all the girls' underpants."

Even the government produced ads asking people to do their part in the war effort. Most striking were posters with bright colors and sensational language that encouraged Americans to ration their food, buy war bonds, and basically perform everyday tasks in support of the war effort.

One such ad asked folks to do their own canning, which we did anyhow, but I am not sure the high crust people did any canning. Most likely they just bought their canned goods.

Another ad depicted a young lady stating, "We can do it!" I also remember the sign with Uncle Sam pointing, with the words "I Want YOU" because it was most visible in our area.

Dad was mustered out of the service in March 1946. He had been assigned as a cook and became a pretty damn good one. He never saw combat, but he served his country admirably and was honorably discharged. Once he came home, however, he never cooked a thing.

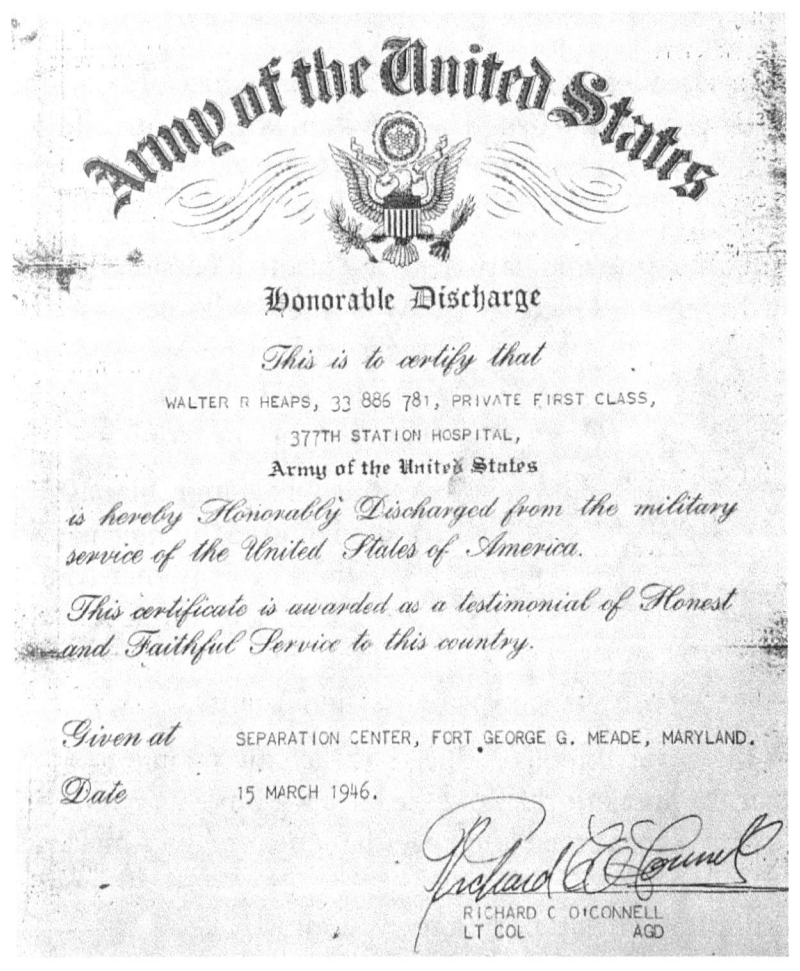

The Farmer Boy's Tale

After Dad returned home, the two-story chicken house he had written Mom about so much became a reality with help from the GI bill. I remember gathering and candling eggs. It seemed like us kids never had much time to play. One time our work horses, Pet and Guy, got loose. They ran around at top speed, kicking up their heels, headed directly toward a ditch where Dale and I were playing. Mom's heart was in her throat, worrying we would get trampled. When both horses swerved and went around us, Mom's heart began beating again. After Pet and Guy became too old for farming, they became our pets.

Me and my brother Dale did build a dam in the creek where we swam in our underwear. But Mom did not like that because she told us she could never get our underwear white again, so most of the time we just swam naked. It seemed to make sense to us.

We roamed around the entire farm and found an old dump in the very back of one of the fields. We used to scrounge along the road and these old abandoned dumps looking for soda bottles people threw away. We took them to the nearest store that would give us the most money.

Certain soda bottles were worth more money than others. When we found them, we felt really lucky. Near the holidays I purchased some cheap Christmas presents and, of course, some penny candy for myself.

Our family had a border collie, Lassie, who was a great dog. She would follow us around and try and herd us back to the front yard so we did not go out into the road.

Upon the recommendation from one of our neighbors, Dad purchased a border collie from a breeder out west. As he put, they had the best "cow dogs." Dale and I could hardly wait for Lassie to arrive. When the time finally came, we all went down to the local rail yard in Woodbine, Pennsylvania, to pick her up. Dale and I had the privilege of naming her Lassie. She became our best friend.

One of our jobs as kids was to separate the roosters from the pullets, Lassie would let the pullets go, but somehow, she knew to keep the roosters in until we caught them. They would become our Sunday dinner.

By that time we had a whole flock of chickens. When the crew came to debeak the pullets, they used what was commonly known as a "debeaking machine." This was a major job, and not a pleasant task. As I remember, it smelled awful.

Most summers we went barefoot until the bottoms of my feet became like shoe leather. I could step on a bee and not even feel the sting. Sometimes we would step on them on purpose.

Dale and I found out the white-headed bumble bee is a male carpenter bee which has no sting. I used to take the carpenter bees and tie a string to them so they wouldn't fly away. They were my play toy. When I wasn't playing with them, I would sit and marvel at them drilling holes in wood, watching the sawdust flying everywhere.

We never had enough money to go around. Granddad used to give my mother ten dollars a year to buy Christmas gifts for all the children. Mostly we kids received new clothes and maybe some oranges and candy.

Granddad always thought clothes, shoes, and maybe an orange or some candies were the best presents for us, but I felt like we should have some "real" gifts. There were only a couple of times when we got anything I considered a *real* present, like the time

Dale and I got a brand-new American Flyer train set and some barnyard animals.

Dad fashioned a train layout out of used plywood. We ran those trains until the wheels practically fell off. That was the best Christmas I remember as a kid.

*I had my train refurbished and now it just sits and collects dust.
But I would not take a million dollars for it.*

Another year my Dale and I got one spinning top to share. Thinking back on it, I am pretty sure it was a used one. When you made the top go round, it sounded like a train the faster it went. Anyhow we wore it out before the holidays were over.

Most every year we got a new pair of engineer boots. Even these were secondhand, but I did not know it at the time. We wore our engineer boots all the time. When we finished our morning chores on the farm, we simply sprayed them off with a garden hose and wore them to school.

They were not popular at school in those times, though, but I kind of liked the look of them and didn't care. I really did not have much choice though, as bare feet were not allowed in school.

Another year we both got a wooden yoyo. I played with mine until I was able to perform certain tricks. One of the tricks I mastered was called "walk the dog." Eventually, the string broke. I used all manner of other string trying to fix it. I even used old baler twine which didn't work too well. By the time I was able to find just the right kind of string, I was on to another phase in my life and the yoyo didn't fascinate me anymore.

One year my brother Dale and I worked all summer mixing cement by hand for Dad and the masons so we could purchase our first three-speed bicycles. We thought we were high crust when we rode them into town to redeem our soda bottles.

Another year we each got a Red Ryder BB gun. The first thing Mom said was, "Don't shoot any robins."

Me with my sister Sharon and brother Dale.

Well, Dale and I both saw this bird sitting on the electric wire and thought we were too far away. Both of us took aim anyway. We shot and the bird fell dead. We were never sure who hit it, but it didn't matter since our mother scolded us both.

When I was five years old, my grandfather passed away. I only remember meeting him once or twice so my memory is vague. He seemed to be a really nice man.

On October 15, 1954, Hurricane Hazel ripped through town and tore the roof off our chicken house. The strongest and only Category 4 hurricane to ever hit the Carolina coast, nineteen people were killed in North Carolina. The damage totals amounted to more than $300 million across the East Coast.

Not long afterwards, Dad sold what was left of the chicken farm. We moved around and rented a lot of houses until 1956 when Dad purchased our 75-acre homestead, right across the road from his father's earlier home.

Charles W. Heaps
(Oct. 22, 1883–Jul. 3, 1946)

When I was 16 years old, my grandmother, Ozella Marie Richardson-Heaps passed away. I thought it was odd she had two last names. Apparently she was ahead of the times because lots of women hyphenate their last name today.

After Granddad's passing she went to live with her daughter and our Aunt Ruth who lived in Joppa, Maryland, at the time. It was a real treat to visit her since it seemed so far away and motor vehicles were not as reliable.

75-Acre Farm...
Our Homeplace

In 1956, when I was 15 years old, my parents bought our 75-acre dairy farm from Uncle Cam and Aunt Helen Reed. It was on a dirt road in a rural town. Being a teenager, I did not care for farm life.

The clapboard farmhouse had no insulation. There was one grate in the middle of the floor for heat that came from an old coal furnace which had to be started every morning.

The house's chimney and metal roof were added later but the rest of it looked the same as this more recent picture.

Of course the house had no air conditioning. In the summer we would to take our mattress out in the yard and get eaten up by mosquitoes… but it was the only way we could find relief from the heat.

In winter, the windows were so drafty that we had to sleep with our clothes on. We used to jump out of bed and go straight to the barn to get warm.

Included in the purchase was an assortment of farm equipment and animals. The 9N Ford tractor was already well-used, but we needed it for farming and other chores.

On weekdays and weekends, I milked cows and did whatever needed to be done around the farm. The farm work was a great deal to expect from a teenage boy who knew nothing about farming, but it taught me a lesson I have carried with me until this day: *I had to work for a living because no one was going to give me anything.*

I enjoyed the smell of the first-cut hay and taking a bath in the creek in the evening. The water was cold at first, but even if we turned blue, my brother Dale and I really enjoyed it. Time seemed to go at a slower pace back then. There wasn't the hustle and bustle of today. But that was about all I enjoyed, as we were as poor as church mice.

One of the most non-profitable of Dad's businesses was when he purchased an old 1949 Chevy flatbed truck.

As fate would have it, one day my aunt wanted Dad to haul her old player piano, which seemed to weigh a ton. As usual, it was up to me and Dale to load it into the truck.

After picking up the piano, we stopped at this little convenience store, and Dad bought us a sandwich and soda pop. Of course he got himself a pack of Camel cigarettes and lit up.

We got back in the truck and were riding along, discussing our adventure while eating and drinking. Out of the blue, this vehicle pulled alongside us, honking the horn and pointing to the back of our truck. When we looked back, we saw the piano in flames. We stopped right away and pulled the piano off before the truck could catch on fire.

For some reason Dale and I got the giggles and we laughed so hard our sides hurt. I am sure my father heard us but he never said a word.

My aunt told us all not to worry about it, but needless to say, we did not haul any more furniture.

When I was in high school, a group of the local Fawn Grove boys decided they would purchase a designed jacket so they could stand out from the crowd. After a lot of discussion, they came up with a name and color. The last thing they found out was that they needed one more person to make enough for the full custom order.

I believe after a lot of reluctance on their part they asked if I wanted to order one. I think it surprised them when I said yes.

After waiting what seemed like an eternity, the jackets finally arrived. When I asked where my jacket was, I was told someone else named Walt had it.

As I was telling Dad about my issue with the jacket, a family friend, Robby Sexton, heard how heartbroken it made me. He asked me who had it. When I told him the boy's full name, he did not say a word.

When he came back later, he had my jacket, and that sure made an impression on me. I vowed no one would ever treat me like that again.

Since neither Dale nor I had a car, on more than one occasion I walked to the nearest gas station to play the pinball machine and possibly buy a soda and maybe split a cupcake. Most of the time we had to walk there and back. but if we were lucky someone would come along and take us home.

One day on the farm, our cousin Herbert, who was Uncle Cam and Aunt Helen's son, along with some of his drunken buddies, stole our 9N Ford tractor. They took it on a rot gut whiskey run to a place about 30 miles away. On the way home, his friend Milky fell off the back of the tractor. No one realized it until they got back home though. When they went out to find him, retracing their route, they found Milky laid out in a ditch with a broken arm.

These same characters finally bought a car of their own. On weekends, they would park it in our lower driveway and drink until all hours of the night.

Soon my brother Dale and I had enough of their antics, so we devised a plan. Over the next couple of weeks, we gathered rocks until we had a nice big heaping pile. The next moonlit Friday when they parked in our driveway, we threw rocks at their car until we broke a couple of windows.

The next week my father asked us, "You boys didn't throw any rocks at their car, did you?" We looked at each other sheepishly and shook our heads. He said, "I didn't think so," and that was the last we heard about it, but those guys never parked their car in our driveway again.

Another crazy car story was when we needed to take a calf to the auction, and had to load it in our family car. First, we had to take out the backseat. Still, the only way the calf would fit in the car was if we stuck its head out the rear window. When we rolled through town, the calf was bellowing its head off. Dale and I laughed so hard our sides were sore.

The old Ford 9N was not big or strong enough to handle all the farm work, so my father bought a newer John Deere "A" tractor with narrow wheels on the front and what I thought were really high rear tires. I never liked that tractor because it sat higher and had those narrow wheels up front. It also had a hand clutch instead of a foot clutch.

I was glad I did not have to use it much, but I do remember one time when I was told to disk the corn field. I had been out the night before and didn't make it to bed. Well, there I was riding along on the tractor and I fell asleep. I was rudely awakened by tree limbs hitting me in the head. The tractor had veered out of the cornfield and into the wooded area alongside the field. Once I finally got the tractor back up out of there, I stopped it and laid down in the grass and took a nap.

One time one of the rear tires on the John Deere "A" tractor went flat. Dale and I needed to figure out how to get the tire off since the jack did not work. Even though we were pretty muscular from working on the farm, we knew there was no way we could lift the tractor high enough by ourselves.

While all this was going on, our Uncle Virgil pulled up. "Go get some blocks," he said. "I'll pick up the tractor by the back spindle. When I get it high enough, you can take the wheel off and put the blocks under the axle."

He backed up to the tractor and grabbed the axle with his bare hands and lifted. We rolled that tractor tire down the embankment and put it on the back of the pickup truck. We might have thought we were muscular, but we only had "show muscle" while Uncle Virgil had "real muscle."

While he was there, Uncle Virgil asked if I wanted to go along to the Pimlico racetrack at some point. I jumped at the idea since I had never been to see the horse races.

When the following Saturday finally came, it was a warm day with a little breeze—the perfect day for horse racing. Uncle Virgil came and off we went. I had a fifty-dollar bill to spend and I put another five dollars in my shirt pocket for lunch.

I don't know if it was just me being excited or what, as I lost all my money, so Uncle Virgil had to buy me a sandwich for lunch.[1]

---

[1] I never went back to the Pimlico track again until recently when I took Kathy to see American Pharaoh race for the triple crown.

Around that time, Dad bought a brand-new New Holland baler, the Hayliner 98, on time payment. Back then New Holland offered financing with little money down and low interest.

Dad saw this as a way to make life better on the farm and also make money. He could hitch the baler to the front of his wagon, and magically, the baled hay or straw would shoot right up out of the baler onto the wagon behind it.

Sometimes it took two men to stack the bales on the wagon as they shot up. It sure beat loading and unloading loose hay by hand with a pitchfork. It was so innovative, other farmers came over to help bale just to see how the machine worked.

It wasn't long until the baler paid for itself through freelance work. Dad charged by the bale and he could finish a good-sized field in a short time compared to doing it the old-fashioned way.

The most profitable business my father and brother got into, however, was buying and selling walnut logs. When the old truck finally gave out, Dad had made enough money to purchase a brand new Ford F 600 truck.

In 1959 during my senior year, the school's Guidance/Ag teacher called me into his office. He explained to me that there was a two-year accounting scholarship available at Goldey Beacon College. I actually thought he must be talking to the wrong kid. He kept persisting though until I finally relented and took the test. To my surprise I won the scholarship.

I had believed since I was not from the upper crust, I wasn't good enough to be offered a scholarship, let alone get one. Before I left for college, Dale told me, "People like us cannot fail no matter what happens."

In the fall semester of 1959, I headed off to Goldey Beacon College in Wilmington, Delaware. I thought I was prepared to leave farm life behind. But imagine a small-town kid going off to college in the big city during the era of free love, race riots, and the whole hippie scene. I was totally unprepared.

Four of the girls in my class invited me and some other boys over to study after school. The one rule of their house was that we had to attempt to do our homework first.

The school had made arrangements for my room and board at Ms. Lacy's house. My responsibilities included planting a garden, mowing the lawn, and doing small jobs around the house.

One night I missed the city bus and had to walk about two miles out of the way. I was used to hitchhiking at home so I thought it wasn't a big deal and stuck out my thumb. A stranger picked me up. When we started driving in the opposite direction from Ms. Lacy's, I had a feeling this was not going to turn out well. As soon as the guy's car stopped at a stop sign, I jumped out and took off on foot!

Later on, I learned Goldey Beacon College gave out one scholarship a year to an underprivileged family. I realized I did not really care if my place in society would never be in the upper crust. I liked being considered the underdog.

After college, I worked as a carpenter's helper during the day and used the money for night school where I took a machine shop course.

My first car-buying experience was when I bought a 1953 Chevrolet. It was nice looking, but when you went downhill and let off the gas, it smoked so bad you could not see the car behind you. I had to resort to going to service stations and getting used oil to put in the motor. It was like a tank.

While I was taking the machine shop course, I met Perry and we became fast friends. Sometimes I would pick him up at his house and we would drive around looking for girls. He had a girlfriend at the time who attended a local school for nursing. We would attend their social parties where there was dancing. I even took a couple of those girls out for a date.

On summer weekends I went swimming at Shinny's or hung around the local drive-in. Once at the swimming pool, I met a nice-looking girl. We got to talking and I found out she was only fifteen. I gave her a quarter and told her, "Call me when you turn sixteen."

One year later, Betsy called me and we dated a couple of times. Later I found out she was on the rebound from a former boyfriend, and they eventually got back together and were married.

Rather than go back home, I rented a room in Ms. Sandy's backyard cottage. She was a single older lady who lived with her boyfriend Bob.

The cottage had a small stove, refrigerator, and some cupboards, though I never cooked anything there. In fact, most mornings I would stop and buy coffee and cupcakes, and in the evenings I stopped at a diner on the way home.

I lost my innocence in that cottage, and I did not even have a chance to enjoy it.

One Saturday night I was awakened. To my disbelief it was Ms. Sandy saying, "My man just got me all worked up and cannot perform."

I needed to go back to the cottage to pick up some clothes I had left behind. Ms. Sandy saw me and said, "I have something pretty horrible to tell you." When I asked her what it was, she said, "Bob hung hisself in my attic."

After the ordeal was over, Ms. Sandy whispered to me, "Would you like to move into the big house with me?" Needless to say, I packed most of my things and moved to Aunt Grace's, though I never did tell my aunt why I wanted to move in so soon.

Not wanting to go back home to the farm, but being a little rattled, or maybe stubborn, I went to see Aunt Grace. She wasn't really my aunt, but our parents had told us to call her that, so I did. I knew she had a big house and periodically kept foster children. I just kind of knew she would take me in because she had been Mom's midwife when I was born.

I didn't even have time to explain why I needed a room because as luck would have it, she had an empty room and welcomed me with open arms. It was a welcome relief to be out of the clutches of Ms. Sandy.

Aunt Grace was a wonderful lady who raised abused foster children. She treated them like they were her own, and while I stayed there, she treated me the same way.

She had a son named Junior who lived with her. He had Cerebral Palsy so bad he could not walk. In fact, he had lain in bed for so long he developed a flat spot on the back of his head.

Basically, all Junior did was sleep and listen to Billy Graham on his little transistor radio. He convinced Aunt Grace if she took him to a revival meeting, he would walk.

One Saturday afternoon I helped her load Junior into her car and she took him to Baltimore to see one of Billy Graham's revival meetings.

Junior got up and crawled to the stage. He never did walk again, but he could get around by crawling, and he did so until he passed away. He was so happy he could at least crawl. He credited his ability to get out of bed because of that revival meeting.

The head of child welfare had been having a hard time locating a foster home for a beaten scared six-year-old boy who had as many emotional scars as visible ones. They came to talk to Aunt Grace as their last hope. Finally she said yes, but told them he would be the last foster child she would take.

When Charlie first arrived, he stood in a corner, afraid of being beaten, or worse—of being scalded with hot water like at home.

After sensing his fear, Aunt Grace convinced him she was not going to allow anyone to hurt him again.

Charlie is now employed at Outback Steakhouse doing odd jobs. He hates to even miss one hour of work. I can only marvel at him because he would never think about taking anything for free from the government or anyone else. He just wants to work for everything he gets. I am glad to have him as a friend.

All told, Aunt Grace took in over 100 foster children, most of whom were special needs. She wasn't able to keep them all, as some eventually returned home. When the state honored her with a citation she simply said, "I only wish I could have raised them all." She was the closest thing I know to Mother Theresa.

During this time, local fire companies would hold square dances. I liked meeting different girls at the dance and asking if they would possibly go out with me. That was how I met Rosie.

On one of our many dates, it was cold and had been snowing. While taking her home in my car, I hit a patch of ice and got thrown from the vehicle. The car, along with Rosie, careened through the guard rail and down a steep embankment. The snowbank was higher than my head except for the route the car took. As I tried to find a way out, I heard Rosie climbing her way up the embankment, crying the whole time.

My 1953 Chevrolet was demolished in this accident. How we both survived, I am not sure!

Insurance covered the accident, and with the money I received, I bought a 1961 Chevrolet Impala two-door three-speed with a 327 V8 engine. It was what's called a "bubble top" because of its unique design.

At another one of those square dances, I met Carole. We saw each other as much as possible, and went to carnivals and even dressed alike.

I got the bright idea I was going to show Carole how to drive even though she did not have her license. We went on the main highway and of course got pulled over by a State Trooper. Carole was wearing a short skirt and the officer could not take his eyes off her legs. Luckily, he only fined me the minimum and he let Carole off easy, delaying her ability to get her driver's license for a month.

By then, Carole's mother could sense things were becoming a little more intense between us. They told her I was too old for her and she could not see me alone anymore–probably because her mother caught us making out on the couch.

After that, I decided to join the Air Force. I passed all the tests and I chose communications. Then came the bad news that I did not pass the hearing test. Just like that, my short stint with the Air Force was over.

I traded my 1961 Chevy in on a 1962 Corvette. It was the prestige image I wanted and needed. It made me feel like I was high crust, and it was what everyone called "scary fast."

We used to close down the main highway so we could race in front of the local drive-in. Not to brag, but the Corvette beat all comers. I had gotten a bit of a reputation and other car owners wouldn't even ask me to race. Other cars could beat the Corvette on the takeoff, but once I got going, it was all over but the shouting.

In 1964, the Beatles took the stage on *The Ed Sullivan Show* in February, and Lyndon Johnson signed the Civil Rights Act into law that summer,

"It is an important gain, but I think we just delivered the South to the Republican Party for a long time to come," Democratic President Johnson purportedly told an aide later that day.

Even with the U.S. entrance to the Vietnam war looming, my focus—right or wrong—was blurred by what happened in my own life.

Witnessing the murder of Harold Dinsmore crowded everything else out of my consciousness.

THE MURDER OF
HAROLD D. DINSMORE

Back in 1958, Harold Dinsmore and his siblings were sent to live with relatives and neighbors when their parents split up. From age thirteen, he worked on the Halstead farm, daylight till dark. He was used to farm life, having helped with the cows, pigs, chickens, and horses on his parents' property.

Life had not been easy for Harold Dinsmore. As a child he had planted crops and helped with the harvesting, cut wood for heating and cooking, helped butcher the pigs each fall, and groomed and watered the horses.

When Harold was eleven, he found an old bicycle frame in the trash and cobbled odd parts together with one of his brothers until they made it usable.

Later on, his parents bought him a three-speed bicycle, the kind with the skinny tires. One day he hooked a rope onto a passing pickup truck. But the plan backfired, and he went flying through the air, along with his bike which hit the roof of the truck.

Harold got hooked up with the wrong crowd and wound up in reform school. Fortunately, his mother and brothers would visit on the weekends. They were allowed to take him shopping to buy new clothes or just out for a drive to get something to eat.

Pennsylvania reform schools in the 1960s housed, trained, and educated adolescents who were delinquent wards of the court. Their mission was to rehabilitate and train juvenile offenders to become productive members of society.

Most housed the boys in dormitory-style conditions. Frequently they would spend half their days in academic endeavors and the other half laboring outdoors as farm help. They also cut Harold's hair shorter than he had ever worn it before.

Boys often ran away from reform school, only to be caught and disciplined, or to return on their own. Violent outbreaks occurred, but were rare.

Harold was eventually released from reform school on three conditions. First, he needed to have a stable job, which he secured as a farm hand at Halstead Farm. Second, he needed to have a stable home in which to live. His aunt, Marie Burton, agreed to sponsor and house him. Third, he always had to be home by midnight.

There was a lot of scuttle-butt among the locals that Harold was part of the "fire bugs" who had been involved in a string of barn fires. But knowing Harold, I never could believe it.

Later Harold worked for the Bata Shoe Company and General Motors, and in 1964 his uncle got him a job at the Chevrolet plant in Baltimore, Maryland.

His girlfriend Glenda Mae called him by the nickname his family used, "Honey." His friends, however, called him "Cigar," because he always seemed to have a cigar in his mouth.

Our lives intertwined on the humid night of Saturday, June 13, 1964, at Jady's Twin Springs Drive-In (which is now named the Delta Family Restaurant).

That fateful evening, Harold Dinsmore ordered food for himself and Glenda Mae. While he waited, he came over to where we all were standing around talking. He joined in, asking us how we were doing and making small talk. He was just that type of guy who would stop by to say hello and ask how you were doing.

Once he got the food, Harold went back out to his car. He handed the items to Glenda Mae then walked to the car behind them. He asked the driver, Richard Wallace, if he would mind moving his car because "I have to be home by midnight."

Mr. Wallace jumped out of his car and a ruckus ensued. The next thing I knew, I was running down the field of uncut grass looking for Harold.

When I found Harold, he was lying bloodied on his back. I estimate that he ran three hundred feet before he fell.

Harold asked me if I would pray for him. I know it sounds dumb, but the only prayer I could think of was one I learned when I was little. "Now I lay me down to sleep. I pray the Lord my soul to keep. If I die before I wake, I pray the Lord my soul to take."

As I was praying, Harold reached out and held my hand. All I could do was hold his hand and wait. I believe we both knew he was not going to make it. I never felt so helpless in my life. I wished I could have done something... anything... to save him.

When the coroner arrived, I helped open Harold's shirt. His chest had been cut by a knife. The deputy coroner, Dr. Hunt, pronounced Harold Dinsmore dead at the scene.

You never know what moment will define your life, but this incident was the one for me. I don't know why Mr. Wallace took offense to Harold asking him to move his car. But I believe Harold is reaching out from the grave to have his story told.

Jail Maryland Man In Delta Stabbing

YORK, Pa. (AP)—Richard E. Wallace, 24, Whiteford, Md., has been charged with murder in the fatal stabbing last Saturday of Harold Dinsmore, 19, Delta; southern York County.

Wallace is a Negro, Dinsmore is white, but authorities said race apparently had nothing to do with the death.

State police said Wallace was charged Sunday before Alderman Chester D. Thomas and confined in the county prison without bail.

They released no details of the stabbing.

Dinsmore's body was found about 11 p.m. along Route 74, about two miles south of Delta, some 20 miles southeast of York.

The Funeral and Trial

After going over the trial transcript, I realized how much seeing Harold's murder affected the rest of my life. In a strange twist of fate, I discovered Harold was killed on his grandfather's original homestead.

His funeral was held on Wednesday afternoon, June 17, 1964, at the Harkins Funeral Home in Delta, and he was buried next to his mother Elizabeth at the Salem Methodist Cemetery. The service was conducted by Paster Walter Whenhold of Slateville Presbyterian.

I couldn't bring myself to attend.

Wallace had been arrested the day following the attack, June 14, and sent to York County Prison, pending bail to be set by the court.

It is possible that race played a part in the anger surrounding this murder, though both men had lost their parents as teens and grew up dirt poor. Harold Dinsmore came from a white family and was raised by an aunt, while Richard Wallace's family was black and he and two of his sisters were sent to live with an uncle after their parents drowned in a flood in 1951.

The charge was filed before Fourteenth Ward Alderman Chester D. Thomas, Jr., by Detective C.J. Shevlin of the Harrisburg police, and the case was prosecuted by District Attorney Daniel Shoemaker. Alderman Thomas indicated he would not set a hearing until Wallace had the chance to get an attorney.

A newspaper account in the *York Dispatch* on June 15, 1964, stated that Harold had died as the result of a single knife blow "during a disagreement involving seven occupants of two cars which pulled into the drive-in." There had been four others in the car with Wallace, two men and two women.

Wallace's attorney, Richard P. Noll, requested a hearing which was granted June 16, after which Wallace was returned to York County Prison, still pending bail to be set by the court.

Another hearing was held on June 25. The court found sufficient evidence to hold Wallace over for trial.

I was later served a subpeona to tesify in court as a witness to the murder. Richard Eugene Wallace was charged with a first count of murder and a second count of manslaughter.

The felony charge was heard in court the next month on July 27, and Wallace pleaded not-guilty. A second defense attorney was Robert W. Morton.

I asked to be seated with the other witnesses during Mr. Wallace's trial. I do remember seeing Mr. Wallace's lawyer coaching him during the proceedings.

The trial had a chilling effect on me. I am not sure why, but the solemnity convinced me even more that I needed to tell what I had witnessed as accurately as possible.

I don't remember exactly in which order I was called to testify, but when I got on the stand, I was as ready as any twenty-year-old could be after witnessing a murder.

I was sworn in by the bailiff, then District Attorney Shoemaker questioned me about everything that happened that night.

> Q: Were you inside the drive-in restaurant at the time Dinsmore walked out?
>
> A: Yes.

Q: How long after that did you exit?

A: About I'd say three to five seconds, about that long.

Q: When you walked out what did you see and hear?

A: I saw Harold jump back like he had been hit or shoved back and then I saw him take a swing at Mr. Wallace and then they got into a real tussle. Mr. Wallace jumped back and drew somewhere, I didn't see where he drew it, I saw it flash when he opened it. I was standing right in line with them from the drive-in and Mr. Dinsmore saw it about the time I did, it looked to me like.

Q: Did he say anything?

A: I couldn't understand. He pointed to it, it looked like he was saying something. I couldn't understand what he said, then he turned around and run. He didn't look like he knew what he wanted to do so he run and Mr. Wallace was right behind him. Then they went around there over behind Mr. Grevis' car and I saw the Dinsmore boy grab hold of Mr. Grevis' car and sort of go back down my sight. I could see Mr. Wallace in above the doorway like.

Q: What did Mr. Wallace do at that point?

A: He just went down, he didn't look to me like he appeared to fall, he went down at him like then they got back up and run around like almost in front of me and turned and went down the field. I saw them go down in the field, then Mr. Wallace ran back up.

There were other witnesses for the Commonwealth, including Glenda Mae who claimed Harold had asked politely and not sworn at Wallace when approaching the other man's car.

Cecilia Davis, who had been in the backseat of Wallace's car with him, testified that Harold had pounded on Wallace's car and used profanity. She claimed that it was Harold who struck the first blow. She also testified that Wallace had admitted killing Harold but she had laughed because she thought he was joking. Then they "took the back roads home to York."

When Wallace took the stand in his defense, he insisted that Harold fell on the knife—which was a switchblade—during the scuffle, and that he had not intended to kill the man.

He gave some background on his life, telling how his parents had drowned in a flood when he was twelve. Wallace and his two sisters had been sent to live with an uncle.

According to *The Gazette and Daily* report, Wallace testified that Dinsmore had "slammed his fist on the hood" and yelled, "Do you mind moving this god damn car so I can get the hell out of here?"

Wallace told the court he got out of the car, from the backseat, and said, "Why did you hit my god damn car like that?" Then he said, "Then he hauled off and hit me on the nose. He came at me again. Then I pulled my knife out. I was scared."

He said Dinsmore told him to put the knife away, but he didn't because "I was scared. I didn't want him to hit me. I wanted him to get away from there so I could get back (in the car) and leave."

According to Wallace, the two of them ran around the car, then "he reached and grabbed me when he slipped—that's when he pulled me over and the knife cut him."

"He fell... got up and ran. I chased him across the highway... he went into a field. I came back." Wallace said he knew Dinsmore was "cut" because he saw blood on his shirt.

When Wallace returned to his car, his nose was bleeding. "All I wanted to do was get him away from my car so I could leave."

When asked during the trial about Dinsmore's death, Wallace said, "I would give my right arm to see that man sitting there, anything."

According to that same article in *The Gazette and Daily*, District Attorney Shoemaker said: "There is sufficient justification in this case for the greatest penalty."

During the final address to the jury, Harold's lawyer, Mr. Morton, pleaded with them "not to snuff out another life."

Before sending the jury out for deliberations, the judge asked Mr. Wallace if he had any last thing to add and I remember he said, "I'll kill every one of you SOBs that testified against me." Then the judge instructed the jury that the sentence should not be "for revenge" but rather to see that justice was done. He made them aware of four possible verdicts: first degree murder, second degree murder, manslaughter, or not guilty.

The jury deliberated from 3:50 until 8:15 P.M. that night, before returning a unanimous guilty verdict. They were sent back for deliberations about the sentence, and at 9:20 P.M. returned with a verdict of "guilty."

Newspaper accounts of the trial stated Wallace showed no emotion when his sentence was pronounced. In a second deliberation, the jury voted to spare him from the electric chair, instead issuing a life sentence.

> "In this case then in which the jury has found you guilty of the offense of murder in the first degree, the sentence of the court is you undergo imprisonment at separate and solitary confinement at hard labor in a state correctional institution to be selected by the Deputy Commissioner for Treatment for and during the term of your natural life, that this sentence be complied with; that you be delivered by the Sheriff of York County or one of his deputies to the Eastern Correctional Diagnostic & Classification Center at Philadelphia, Pennsylvania there to be dealt with according to law, this being the sentence that has been decreed by the jury that tried the case."

A motion was made to file an appeal, but on Monday, October 26, 1964, Wallace's attorneys Noll and Morton requested to withdraw the motion after the following interview.

The judge asked Wallace directly if he understood the implications of this action.

> Q: Do you understand what that means?
>
> A: Yes sir.
>
> Q: What does it mean?
>
> A: That there is not enough legal grounds for another trial. I think everything has been gone over.
>
> Q: It is your wish as well as their advice to you, is this correct?
>
> A: Yes sir.

Morton went on to say, "Mr. Wallace indicated to me that the first trial having been such an emotional situation for him he doesn't desire to go through a new trial again in any way, shape or form." The judge once more affirmed this with Wallace directly. Then he asked if Wallace had anything else to say before his sentence was imposed.

> "Your Honor, I am not too good at words. There are a few things I would like to say. I feel as though I had two of the best lawyers in York and I think that they did everything they possibly thought was right. The reason I don't want to go through this new trial I think everything has been gone over thoroughly and I'd hate to put them through the same thing again."

The judge then permitted the withdrawal of the motion for a new trial.

The following notice appeared in the *York Daily Record* on October 27, 1964.

Man Found Guilty Of First Degree Murder Imprisoned For Life

Richard E. Wallace, 24, Whiteford, Md., found guilty of first degree murder Aug. 25 by a York county jury, was sentenced yesterday to life imprisonment in a state correctional institution for the fatal stabbing of Harold Dinsmore, 19, Delta, on June 13.

The sentence was imposed by Judge George W. Atkins after defense counsel withdrew a motion for a new trial and the defendant pleaded guilty.

"I think everything has been gone over thoroughly," Wallace told the court, "and I don't want to go through it again."

According to testimony at the trial, Dinsmore's death followed an argument at Jady's Twin Springs drive-in, Delta RD 2.

An article on October 31, 1964, in *The York Gazette and Daily* noted that Judge George W. Atkins approved the payment of $1,520 to Wallace's attorneys for the trial, covering costs of $750 each plus $20.25 to a stenographer. The attorneys had been court-appointed after Wallace filed a petition claiming he was indigent and unable to afford counsel.

A further $142.50 was approved as payment to private detective Richard P. Sneeder for work as a special investigator while Wallace's defense was prepared.

The case against Wallace was later taken to the Supreme Court of Pennsylvania to determine whether the lower court made a mistake in denying the petition for a new trial without a hearing. The matter was argued on May 25, 1967, and an opinion was issued by Justice Roberts on September 26 of that year. The court supported the earlier decision, stating:

> "In the face of his responses to the court's questioning, we cannot accept appellant's suggestion that he did not realize the consequence flowing from the withdrawal of the post-trial motions. Had he utilized his absolute right to appeal, he undoubtedly would have requested this Court to grant him a new trial. Yet he specifically informed the court below that he believed 'there is not enough legal grounds for another trial,' and expressed complete satisfaction with the manner in which his attorneys had conducted his trial."

I recently found a copy of the settlement for Harold's "estate," which was filed in the Orphans' Court of York County by his aunt, Marie Burton, who paid $915 for Harold's funeral. His sole asset was listed as his 1955 Pontiac convertible, valued at $395.

AND NOW TO WIT: *August 29,* 1964, upon presentation of the foregoing petition and consideration thereof by the Court, the Court does hereby allow and set aside to Marie D. Burton, Aunt of Harold Dinsmore, deceased, the following personal property:

    1955 Pontiac Convertible

    Mfr's. No. W855H16424

    Title No. L11319146

the same being awarded to her in kind, and the following refunds:

    Automobile Insurance, Nationwide Insurance Co., Check No. A58566799 in the amount of $47.70

    Refund from U. S. Treas Dept., Withholding Tax - $104.38

    Refund from Maryland State, Income Tax - $10.45

as reimbursement toward the payment of the burial expenses of the said decedent, and she is hereby authorized to endorse title to the same for the purpose of completing any transfer and endorse any checks or orders received on account of said refunds, and the same shall be done without appraisement and without notice.

                        By the Court

                        Richard E. Kohler

LIFE MOVES ON

After the trial it seemed like I just ran around not caring. I no longer needed the Corvette as a crutch so I traded it for an orchid colored 1965 Chevelle Malibu SS four-speed.

During this time, I met Sandi, a good-looking girl from the area. We dated a couple of times and one night she told me she was going to the beach for a week and asked if I wanted to come along. Of course, I said yes, but I soon found out the real reason she had asked me. Her parents were going along and they needed a reliable car for the trip. As you can image, I did not have a good time. When we got back home, I never saw her again. I did not like feeling like I had been used.

On a lazy Sunday afternoon, a friend of mine and I were just hanging out at Jady's Twin Springs Drive-In when we both witnessed this good-looking girl come sashaying into the restaurant. I bet him a dollar I could get a date with her.

I succeeded, but she lived in the city, a good distance off. On the date, I sent my brother Dale up to take her out, pretending to be me, since we looked similar.

They went to the drive-in and he pulled out a cigarette and started smoking. Right away she knew something was up because I did not smoke. He finally had to admit that he was my brother… but he actually got another date with her as himself.

Another time I had a date scheduled with two different girls on the same night. One was for 6:00 P.M. and the other at 11:00 P.M.

Eventually I settled down a little and landed a pretty good job at Bowen-McLaughlin (now BAE) thanks to my machine shop training, but it was on the second shift which curtailed my partying.

One night I decided I would eat in their cafeteria. On the way home I came down with food positioning and had to be taken to the hospital. Thank goodness it was a Friday night and I had the weekend to recuperate. I went to work on Monday morning and I never ate in that cafeteria again.

Another time I knelt down to pick up a piece of material to put into my machine. I heard something pop in my left knee. After that, I could hardly walk for the next couple of days. I had to have an operation for a torn cartilage.

The company said it was not work related. I was laid up for six weeks with no income, so I went home to the farm until I could recover. Once I was able to work, I quit working for Bowen-McLaughlin.

MEETING KATHY

Out of the blue, a friend called and asked if I wanted to go roller skating. I told him, "There won't be any girls there," and he replied, "You never know."

To my surprise, when we arrived, there was a local church group there with a lot of girls!

Kathy, senior year, 1967.

I remember leaning against a pole when a girl from the church group came by and grabbed me around the neck. She almost knocked me over. I looked at her and said, "If you want to make out, let's go outside to the car." I didn't see her again the rest of the night.

Later I learned this girl named Kathy had not known how to stop on skates, so she had grabbed the nearest solid thing she could find to help stop her. Me.

I had ridden past her farm several times over the years, and every single time she waved at me. When I asked her about it later, she replied, "I wave at everyone who waves at me." So maybe I wasn't as special as I thought.

Later that year, I was at the local swimming pool when some of the guys announced that they were going horseback riding. I decided to go find them after I got bored at the pool.

Along the way I saw a little sign along the road which read "Horseback Riding." Just then, I looked up into the field and saw that same girl wave at me. I honked my horn and kept going to find the rest of the guys.

When I got to the place where they rented horses, the gentleman there said they were all out and would not be back for some time. Rather than wait around, I decided to go back where I had seen that girl waving.

It was Kathy.

Kathy and I dated for about a year and on December 25, 1966, I hid an engagement ring in a toy horse box.

Kathy loved horses but a toy was not the kind of present she was looking for. Even though I could see her disappointment, she acted as though that horse was wonderful. She was about to throw the box away when I told her to take a closer look.

Kathy has said I never really asked her to marry me. All I know is I remember saying, "I DO," at the wedding, and we have been together ever since.

When Kathy finally located the ring. Mom laughed and told her there is no returns on this merchandise.

We were married the next summer, on Saturday, July 29, 1967. At the time, Kathy was not old enough to be married in Pennsylvania without parental consent, so we were wed in Maryland.

There were about 70 people, with relatives and friends from both sides of the family in attendance.

Kathy and I planned to go to Niagara Falls for a short but memorable honeymoon. We hoped we would get enough cash from the wedding gifts to help pay for some of the trip. As it turned out, we got more than enough money.

After the ceremony, dinner and unwrapping all the gifts, we went back to Kathy's house and changed out of our wedding clothes. Then we headed out on what we felt would be a pretty long trip to the falls.

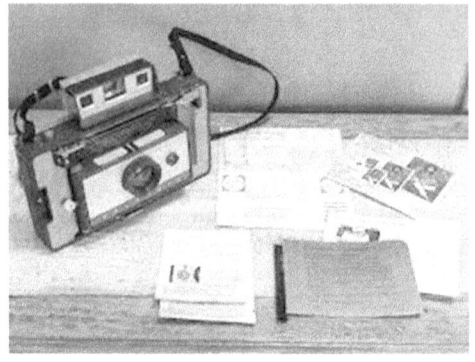

In 1965, Polaroid released their latest version of their camera called "the swinger" which caught the attention of the younger generation. The catchy song "Meet the Swinger" by Barry Manilow, starring

Ali McGraw, provided the fuel in making Polaroid a household name.

One of our most unexpected wedding gifts was one of those fancy new Swinger Polaroid cameras. We made good use of it during our honeymoon trip.

When we got on the road, we drove for a couple of hours but decided it was time to stop and get a good night's sleep. Enter "Little Bo Sheep" motel. It was the perfect place to spend the night—not fancy, but the owners were nice and the place was very clean.

We slept in on Sunday. After breakfast we were on the road to our destination which wasn't far. We decided to go to the Canadian side of the falls. We found a comfortable hotel near there and decided to head out on our adventure.

Kathy caused quite a ruckus while taking pictures. Apparently, no one had seen one of those cameras before and they were excited to see how it worked and to look at the pictures it took.

Our first journey was on the Maid of the Mist boat ride, which went under the falls. We both got soaking wet as the boat

ducked under the falls, then turned around and came back out again. We had to go back to our hotel and change clothes.

That afternoon we went to the famous gardens with the floral clock.

On Monday morning after breakfast, we went on the walk under the falls. This time they gave us each raincoats and slippers. Unfortunately, we got soaked once again and had to go back to change clothes at our hotel.

After lunch we just roamed around and took in the local Canadian flavor. We both thought this might be our first and last trip to Canada.

On Tuesday after breakfast we went back to the American side of the falls. We both were a little disappointed. There seemed to be more to do on the Canadian side and it had just felt cleaner there, so we decided we would check out the next morning and head back home. Of course on the way we stopped at the same Little Bo Sheep motel. Since this was our first trip away from home, we both were glad to return.

MAKING A HOME

Back in Pennsylvania after the honeymoon, we rented a third-floor apartment in York city. The electric, heat, and trash were included in the monthly rent.

Kathy had won a scholarship to attend a college secretarial course. She started her classes and I started my job as an insurance agent in the city.

Soon afterward, Kathy confided in me that she was overwhelmed. She felt she wanted to go back to the bank. After a long discussion and me insisting that she made sure they would hire her back.

She returned to the bank the following Monday. We lived on my earnings and saved hers in anticipation of building our house on a plot of land her parents had promised when we announced our wedding date.

Times were tough as Kathy and I still struggled with expenses. She had wanted to be a stay-at-home Mom, but took a job at McCrory's as an accounting clerk while her sister babysat our daughter.

In May 1969 there was localized rioting and looting in the city of York. The mayor, John L. Snyder, had served in his position during the 1940s and most of the '60s, and approved of the police using dogs to subdue civic unrest.

The previous summer, in July 1968, about 50 black youths assembled in Penn Park. When a rock bounced off a police cruiser, the officer fired a shot into the air, setting off the violence. Two more events in August and September pitted whites against blacks.

By the summer of '69, York was a seething cauldron of hatred. Dozens of people were injured and two even died—one white police officer named Henry Schaad, and a black woman from South Carolina named Lillie Belle Allen who was visiting family in the area.

On July 22, 1969, National Guard troops rolled into town and Gov. Raymond P. Shafer declared a state of emergency.

The Farmer Boy's Tale

That same year the famed Woodstock festival took place, and Pontiac rolled out the Firebird Trans Am.

My job was at Washington National Insurance, selling and collecting weekly life and accident insurance. They were always pushing for more sales and pitting me against other agents. On top of that, they always transferred the worst-paying customers to the new person, so this meant I had to spend a lot of money on gas, trying to find the person to get them to pay their premiums.

Because of the strain, I decided to go back to working in a machine shop. I got a job at Allis-Chambers (now Voith). They promised I would only be on night shift for about six months, but that was just a promise they never intended to keep.

With all the chaos going on in York, Kathy and I decided to get out of dodge. We rented a small house while our first home was being built.

Dad and my brother Dale did all the work to build that house, not using even one sub-contractor. I took a week off and helped them build our three-bedroom, one bath house.

The thing that amazed me about Dad was how he could look at the lay of the land and picture the exact way our house would fit into the landscape... and it all came out the way he said it would.

I was able to charge materials at the lumber houses to my father's name and get his discount. A lumber company in the city had a fire shortly after we started building, so Dale and I took Dad's 1966 Ford flatbed truck and brought home materials from the fire sale, along with anything Dad had ordered to use the next day.

We were proud of our home and the way it was built.

On Thursday, July 3, 1969, our daughter Christina was born, earlier than expected. As we were going to the hospital, I asked Kathy if she was sure it wasn't just false labor. Chris was born shortly after we made it to the hospital. She just wanted to get on with life. We often referred to her as our "firecracker." She was a beautiful baby with the prettiest black hair.

Around six months of age, our daughter started having problems with her ears. Her ears were tubed so many times she started reading lips because she couldn't hear what people were saying. Luckily, most of her school teachers were considerate enough to seat her in front of the class.

We did not have a lot of money during those days, so instead of going out to the movies or the drive-in, we went back to the farm on the weekends. Of course we took Chris with us, and my three sisters used to dress her up and play with her and treat her as another sister.

Around 1971, Kathy quit her job at the bank and went to work for the local school district.

One particular Saturday morning, I was talking with Dad, explaining to him how unhappy I was with my present job. He said, "I heard Bechtel Corporation's hiring at Peach Bottom. With your background, why don't you give 'em a call?"

I was a little apprehensive, but he added, "Nothing ventured, nothing gained," so I called and got an interview for the following Monday. I guess it went well since they hired me and I started my new job as junior accountant the following week.

Once our income increased, the expenses seemed less worrisome. I worked my way up from junior accountant to senior accountant. I balanced the payroll and proved out the company bookkeeping by hand.

One of my many jobs back then was to pick up the mail at the post office and bring it back to the office to be sorted. This was no small feat. I'm talking three or four big canvas sacks of mail each daily!

Once my boss and others asked me to pick up lunch for them at a local delicatessen while I was out. Then others in the building started asking me to pick up their lunch, too. Instead of calling ahead, they would give me a list. Sometimes it would take over an hour until I could get back to work. I thought this was a strange set-up, but I didn't want to make waves and so I didn't say anything.

I worked my way up and became a senior accountant responsible for balancing the payroll and all the company's books. There weren't any computers yet, so I had to prove the payroll, general ledger, and everything manually.

At some point Kathy and I decided Chris needed a playmate. We thought about adoption, but that was a lengthy and difficult process. Then by a stroke of luck we heard of a program called the Fresh Air Fund. Basically, it meant we could take a child from New York City and bring them to the country to stay for the summer.

We were paired with a beautiful young girl named Laurie Duchene. We all fell in love with her the minute we met Laurie and her sponsor at the bus depot. She had what we thought was this funny New York accent, but by the end of the summer, she talked just like us… until the following year when it started all over again.

We put a fan in Laurie's bedroom window so it wouldn't be so hot. The very first night she got up and came into our bedroom crying. When we asked what was wrong, she said, "It's too dark." As we installed a night light, she asked if we could remove the fan and lock all her windows, which we did.

After a couple of nights, Laurie told us it was all right to put the fan back in, and she said we could unlock the windows. Once her fears settled down and the room was cooler, she slept a whole lot better. Laurie never asked to remove the fan again.

Since she had brothers and sisters back home, she fit right in with all our extended families. We took her everywhere we went. You might say Laurie became our adopted child, at least for several summers.

Laurie would come to visit even when she got too old to be sponsored, and we paid her way down and back from New York City. She is now married and has two sons. One is a fireman who was out sick the day the twin towers were hit in New York City or else he would have been involved in that unfortunate incident.

As the Bechtel job at Peach Bottom was winding down, I was one of the last ones to leave. The way things worked with Bechtel was that whenever a job was complete, you either went with the company to another location or you had to find another job.

My boss told me I was being transferred to Limerick, Pennsylvania, to be their Accounts Payable Supervisor. The company would move us, all expenses paid, and they would also help sell my house. I had no idea where Limerick was, but it was a promotion and I would be earning more money, so Kathy and

I decided I should make the two-hour commute (each way) for a while to see how things would go.

When I arrived at the new position, I found file cabinets full of invoices. I was the supervisor of four people whose sole job was to pay these invoices. Each invoice had to match up with a purchase order and the corresponding receiving materials report before it could be paid. Then I had to initial the payment form before the check could be cut.

One day my supervisor told us that Bechtel had landed this massive job in Saudi Arabia. They were looking for volunteers. He said the salaries were great, but you had to commit to stay for three years.

Soon afterward, I noticed people leaving the Limerick site in droves. I knew it wouldn't be long until they asked me to move to Saudi Arabia, too.

After discussing it with Kathy, we decided we wanted to raise our children here in the United States, not halfway across the world. I had worked for Bechtel for ten years, but it was time to find a job closer to home.

New House, New Job, New Child

One day while I still was working at Bechtel, I got a call from Kathy about an ad she had seen in the local newspaper. A 20-acre farmette was for sale. It had a nice barn and it even came with a Farmall B cub tractor. We sold our house and bought it.

It took a while to locate a job that paid anywhere close to what I had been making at Bechtel, until I finally interviewed at Caterpillar Corporation. I was on second shift, working from three until eleven each night. If I got up early, we could work around the farm until I had to leave for my shift. Neither one of us liked me working nights, but I was earning good money so we made the best of it.

Officially, I was an accounting clerk, but actually my job amounted to keeping track of how many pieces each employee could produce in an eight-hour shift. They used a timecard method to keep track of parts produced and how long it took.

Toward the end of each shift, I would collect the timecards with the number of pieces written on it from each person. Then I input their information into a computer before the shift ended. The hardest part of the job was learning to use a computer for the first time.

Hurricane Agnes struck in June 1972, bringing floods and destruction to most of Pennsylvania. Emergency sirens wailed. No one was expecting the floodwaters since the weather forecast had only been for potential light rain. Agnes had been a tropical storm down in Florida and caused only minor damage there before heading back out into the Atlantic. But when the storm made landfall again in southeastern New York, it brought heavy rain.

The U.S. Army Corps of Engineers had constructed a dike system along the Susquehanna River back in the 1940s with 13- to 15-foot levees after a terrible flood in 1936. Agnes's torrential downpour brought rain for close to a week. Water levels surpassed even the 35-foot barriers, and became one of the costliest and most devastating natural disasters in the state.

Kathy was working as a secretary for a local builder and was allowed to bring our daughter Chris to work with her. Of course, as the water rose quickly, Kathy made the frightful decision to forge the high waters all the way home. That was something I became used to after living with Kathy; to say she is a little stubborn is putting it mildly.

On Sunday, May 2, 1976, our second child was born, Walter Nathan Heaps. This time I did not say anything to Kathy about it being false labor. I just loaded her up and headed for the hospital.

Of course, this was all happening in the middle of the night. I didn't stop at the first red light or the second one as I could see there was nothing coming. But I didn't notice the police cruiser.

When the officer pulled us over, we explained the situation. He told Kathy to get in his car and instructed me to follow them, but to obey all the stop signs and red lights.

I thought to myself that he was a good one to talk because he went straight through the next several lights with his siren blasting.

I only reached the hospital just as Nathan was about to be born. When they asked if I wanted to be in the delivery room I was flabbergasted. After getting all suited up, I was able to witness my son's birth. What a miracle!

Little did we know what he had in store for us. In years to come, we would become so much more aware how much of a miracle Nathan would turn out to be.

When you live on a farm, there are always "projects" to be done. We first filled in the driveway and leveled it with dirt from the banks. The home was green when we bought it, so we painted the aluminum siding tan and covered the eves with brown coil stock.

To make the house more temperate in summer and winter, we did a number of renovations. First, we cut a hole in the roof and installed a fan for ventilation. We also dug out the basement and poured a concrete pad for a dual-purpose wood/coal stove. The stove needed a chimney, so we built one on the side of the house.

If that wasn't enough, we installed a half-bath upstairs in the home, and added a set of steps inside the house.

We also had projects related to the barn. We needed to replace the roof, and afterward we had the barn painted red. We fixed a stall there for Chris's horse, and made a place under the overhang for Kathy to park her car.

One of our more memorable projects was cutting firewood. We would pack up the children along with an uncooked loaf of bread. Kathy put the dough on the manifold of the truck to raise. Then I would cut the firewood and she and the kids would throw it in the back of the truck bed. When the bread was ready, we had it for lunch with butter and jam. Boy, was that good!

The kids had a horse, a dog, chickens, and a couple of ducks for pets.

There was always mowing and other heavy chores to be done on the farm, so I sold the Farmall B and bought a Ford 9N tractor. I also bought a sickle bar mower to attach to the tractor so I could mow the pasture.

I fashioned a seat and fastened it onto the rear fender well of the tractor. I could strap Nathan into that seat while I mowed, hauled firewood, or whatever else I was doing. He never said a word.

Once we had the wood stove set up in the basement, we cut the fence rows back and burned wood in the stove. But then we had a couple of chimney fires, so since the stove was dual-purpose, we started burning coal instead. We could open the basement door and that stove would heat the whole house.

Chris cared for her own horse and took it to horse shows. When she was twelve years old, she and her 2500-pound horse were winning ribbons. Looking back, it was the best thing we could have done for her.

Nathan used to ride around the farm on his bicycle. He liked playing with the dog and building dams in the stream—all the normal boy stuff.

One day he told Kathy he saw a snake. "How do you know it's a snake," she asked. He replied, "It went *hiss* at me."

When he was around nine years old, Nathan had a serious bike accident and his front teeth got knocked out.

One winter a heavy snowstorm came with a coating of ice on top. Both children decided it would make good sledding. Unfortunately, on the first trip they slammed straight into the fence.

I decided to take the tractor and make tracks in the snow in hopes of slowing them down. On their next trip, they both flew off the sled. We couldn't find Nathan right away.

When we did, we discovered he had broken his wrist. He didn't cry and said it didn't hurt. We ended up taking him to the doctor the following Monday. He had to have a cast which he wore proudly and got everyone to sign.

The farm was a great place to raise our children.

Strange Occasions

One night, for no particular reason, I parked my car up at the barn overnight. The next morning when I went out to go to work, there was a woman I had never seen before sitting inside my car.

I noticed she had a washtub full of clothes in the backseat.

Naturally I asked her what she was doing. She said she was leaving home and wanted me to take her to her boyfriend's house.

I explained to her that I had to go to work and couldn't take her to see her boyfriend.

When I asked her who she was, she told me her name was Edna Trimble. She lived on the next road over from our place, so I took her back to her home and never saw her again.

Another neighbor once called and asked if I would come over since they wanted to cut firewood along our fence line. I agreed and while discussing the situation with the neighbor couple, the wife, Pam, started moving her lips, mouthing the words, "Call me" to me, all while her husband Albert was right there.

I did call to find out what she wanted because she might have been living with some domestic violence issue and need help. But instead she said she had been trying to get my attention for weeks by driving and walking by our house. I just told her I was married and not interested.

A few weeks later Pam called again. "Albert hung himself in the basement." She went on to say that now that she was free, she would like to see me.

I flashed back to the time when Ms. Sandy had told me "Bob hung hisself in the attic." For a third time, I was faced with someone's death. I told Pam I was married and not interested. This time, I never heard from her again.

When I was 35 years old, Granddad Carico passed away. He was the granddad I knew the most. In fact I was one of the pallbearers at his funeral. He operated a turkey farm for several years and had modern equipment like a defeathering machine.

As teenagers Dale and I would help kill and dress turkeys for him to sell over the holidays. It was not a pleasant experience but we did it because he was our granddad.

When I was 50 years old my step-grandmother passed away. Nanny Clyde Higgins-Carico (1894-1991) was not my maternal grandmother but since I knew her best I considered her my real grandmother. At her death, her immediate family took over and our family was excluded from the services. It left a real bitter taste in my mouth.

WESTWARD BOUND

When Chris was twelve and Nathan was only five, we decided to take a family trip out west. It was July 1981, and before leaving home, we thought it might be good to test the camper for a night. The trial run out on the farm allowed us to iron out the bugs. This was beneficial as we discovered items we needed to purchase for the trip.

Both children were instructed on their duties. Chris's job was to snap the canvas down around the spools under each side of the bed. Nathans's job was to find a place for the crank so we could raise and lower the camper when we arrived at our campsite. They both did an excellent job that first night.

We decided we would mostly camp in the National Park system. As a special treat, we would add in some KOA campgrounds which had more amenities. Kathy set up the itinerary, and even booked a rafting trip for one day.

We knew we were setting out on an arduous journey, but thought we were well prepared.

On Friday, July 3, we packed up and headed to Madison, Wisconsin. This was about a twenty-hour drive and we did not arrive at the KOA campsite until the wee hours of Sunday morning following the Independence Day holiday.

We all slept in late because we were exhausted from the drive. When we finally woke up, we had bug bites all over our bodies. Apparently we had not closed up the camper completely the night before. We tried an old remedy of putting damp baking soda on the bug bites. It helped... or at least we thought it did.

On Monday, I was not impressed with the Wisconsin Dells. We decided to stay the night anyhow and head toward Mitchell, South Dakota, the next day.

The Corn Palace was like nothing I had ever seen. The entire building was covered with different types of corn.

On Wednesday, we headed for the Badlands in South Dakota. It was easy to tell why it was called the "badlands." It seemed like the mountains just sprang up and they looked foreboding.

The next day we took in the sights at Mount Rushmore. What an incredible feat it must have been to carve the presidents' faces out of solid rock!

We rode the Black Hills Railroad. They must not believe in guardrails in the west, because I would have sworn we were going over the side a couple of times.

Friday, July 10 took us to The Needles in South Dakota. We were glad we did not have a bigger camper, as it could've easily gotten hung up there. Luckily, we made it without a cinch.

After so much driving, on Saturday we spent the day relaxing. I panned for gold in French Creek, South Dakota. Dumb me wore flip flops and the tops of my feet got sunburned through the water. It was painful to walk for several days afterward. Once again, we used wet baking soda as a treatment.

Saturday took us into the Rocky Mountains. Before that, we thought we had seen mountains in Pennsylvania, but from then on, we decided to call the Appalachian Mountains "hills."

We spent a couple of nights there before heading out for Little Big Horn National Park. On Tuesday, our guide took us right down into the fields where General Custer was killed. After looking at the lay of the land, I came to the conclusion that even though Custer had been a General, he sure didn't make a wise decision about choosing that site to fight the Indians.

There wasn't much else to see around that venue, so we headed for Devil's Tower on Wednesday. You could see the tower rising out of the ground for miles before you actually reached it. This was yet another example of nature so surprising that until you see it, you wouldn't believe it. Rock climbers really enjoy scaling Devil's Tower.

Our Thursday stop was Cold Strip, Montana, where we would visit friends. Al and Chris Durand lived there. Al informed me that my old boss, Jim Wagner, lived nearby. Al and I went to visit him, but he really wasn't himself.

Jim had a brain tumor and his speech was slurred. I'm not even sure he remembered me. I heard shortly after our visit he had an operation and retired. There was some speculation that the only reason he kept his job was so his Social Security income would be higher once he retired.

After a short visit we headed for our next stop, the Big Sky Campgrounds, on Friday, July 17.

It was the first water slide we had ever seen. Of course, Chris and Nathan wanted to try it out right away. They were so in love with that water slide that we had to go find them for dinner. Just as soon as they finished the meal, they went back on it until dark.

Kathy and I wanted to tour Yellowstone National Park on Saturday and maybe Sunday. We started to close camp up a little early. Then it hit us… we could not find the camper crank! Without that little device, we simply could not close up the camper. We made the decision not to say anything to the children so as not to spoil their fun.

We left the camper all the way up and let it sit at the campsite while we toured Yellowstone. We saw Mammoth Springs, Yellowstone River, and the jewel of the trip, Old Faithful, which spouted at the exact time it was supposed to.

That night we got back late to camp, ate supper, and crawled into bed. On Sunday, we got up late but the children wanted to ride on the water slide again.

Instead of touring more, Kathy and I took a much needed rest while the kids played. We discussed the crank issue and decided I would drive 90 miles to the nearest big town on Monday to try to have a crank made, while she would stay at the campground with the children.

As we were getting ready for bed, Nathan heard us talking about the crank. "I know where it is," he told us. Lo and behold, he had put it up on a shelf. He knew exactly where the crank had been that whole time. We just hadn't asked him.

After all that drama, we slept in on Monday and let the kids play one more day on the water slide since we didn't have to have a new crank made.

The next morning we were off again to the Grand Tetons. This was our appointed day and time for the Snake River raft ride. They had these big rubber innertubes that held eight people.

The guide informed us we would be going through some rough rapids. "You'll need to hold on to the ropes on the side of the tube."

As we floated down the smooth part of the river, we saw an eagle just sitting on a tree limb watching us. We also saw a mink and all kinds of butterflies. It was a great experience, but we learned we wouldn't have needed to make a reservation... After our ride concluded, our guide told us about a woman who had fallen off her raft at the rapids recently and had to be rescued.

In the Tetons we took a breathtaking trail ride on horseback. Kathy loved it, but I came back with a sore rump. Afterward, they had a surprise chuck wagon jamboree with a meal. We decided to attend. The singing was great and the food was delicious. We were glad we did not have to cook an evening meal for once.

On Friday morning we headed for Bryce Canyon. What a sight! We found out they offered a trail ride with a packed lunch into the canyon. Everyone except Nathan could take the tour, since he was still quite young. They had a daycare service where they watched Nathan until we returned. Chris was barely old enough and could have stayed, but she wanted to go so we let her.

I told Kathy I would hold the camera and take pictures for us. It didn't take too long on the horse until I gave up that job!

Bryce Canyon is about 8,300 feet deep and the trail down into it is narrow and steep. My horse wanted to stay on the outside of the trail. When I asked the guide about it, he said it was so other people could still walk on the trail next to us. Of course there weren't any guardrails so I spent the whole time holding onto the saddle horn for dear life.

We stopped at the bottom and ate the lunch that was provided. As we started back out of the canyon, the trail led up to an archway made of stone. Once we reached it, I swear my horse made a sharp right turn and its body went halfway out over thin air. I thought for sure we were doomed!

We got up early on Tuesday and headed out for Arizona. When we finally reached the Grand Canyon, we spent the night and went to visit it the next day. They were offering walking tours plus an overnight trip into and out of the canyon—riding a donkey. We made the decision *not* to take the tour, so we spent a couple of hours there before heading out to Salt Lake, Utah, where we visited the Great Salt Lake and also saw the Mormon Temple.

The campsite happened to be close to an orchard with the biggest black cherries, ripe for the taking. We thought about swimming in the Salt Lake but it stunk so bad and there were black flies all over it. We just waded in so we could say we did.

That night I ate so many cherries I almost made myself sick. The next morning we headed out on Monday for the Taylor River in Colorado. I am not sure why they called it a river because back home in Pennsylvania it would be no more than a stream. I purchased a three-day fishing license and I caught enough fish for supper that night. It was delicious.

When we tried to turn on the heater in the camper that night, it would not work, so we snuggled into our sleeping bags as best we could.

That night we woke to someone hollering, "Mommy!" We found Nathan sitting on the ground, still in his sleeping bag. He had just rolled out of his bed.

Needless to say, we didn't get much sleep that night. It was so cold we woke to ice in our plastic cups. As Kathy made breakfast, I started the car heater and put the kids inside until they could get warm.

Then we took off for Dodge City, Kansas. We pulled into our campsite in the wee hours of Wednesday morning. The next day, we went to a show at the Long Branch Saloon where the performers chose kids from the audience to help the sheriff catch the "bad men." Nathan was chosen but we were not so sure he enjoyed being part of the performance. They did a lot of hollering and shooting off their guns.

Thank goodness we went to bed early that night. During the wee hours, Kathy woke me. "We have to leave immediately!" The camper was shaking from a furious wind. Since Kansas is known for its tornadoes, we gathered up the children and put them in the Jeep, then broke camp as fast as we could and headed out of there.

On Thursday evening, we got in late to our KOA campground in Virginia. It was all we could manage just to make dinner and get to bed.

Friday, July 29 was our last day on the road. It had been a long but enjoyable trip. Kathy and I both swore that if we ever went out west again… we would fly.

BANK BOUND

In 1983, I got laid off from Caterpillar. As a union shop, everything went by seniority and I was low man on the totem pole.

After that I held several part-time jobs. One involved working with Dad as a carpenter's helper while he built a house for Paul Peak, the president of Forest Hill State Bank.

One day that bank president asked if I would be willing to come work for him at the bank. He explained the position would start as an outside sub-contractor, shifting their manual accounting system into a computerized one. Once that project was done, he had plans for me to become full-time and be in charge of a whole new department known as the General Service department.

One of my many duties was to organize the numerous forms the bank used. This process took about three months to complete. Another part of my duties was to be responsible for the couriers. I also had to type up the monthly list of expenditures, so I took night classes to learn how to type.

The courier's job was to take inter-office correspondence and deliver currency to other bank locations. After one of the couriers had a serious car accident and money scattered everywhere, I insisted we hire an armored vehicle service to cover this most dangerous part of the job.

Around 1989, Paul asked if I wanted to attend a three-year course at University of Maryland's school of banking. I took that as a request, so off to banking school I went.

The first year I was there, we were unable to stay on campus, so we ultimately stayed at a local hotel. The very first morning we discovered the windshield of one student's car had been broken out overnight.

My second year there, a group of us decided to go out to the local pub. When we started to leave. we were told by police that we needed to stay. When we asked why, they informed us there had been a shooting in the parking lot and one individual had died. We were all a little blurry-eyed as we made it to class the next morning after staying out so late.

The third year, everything went as expected and I graduated.

Just as at Bechtel, sometimes I was asked to do things that weren't exactly in the job description. One day Paul asked if I would take a ride with him to look at a stove down in Rising Sun, Maryland, so off we went. I began to wonder where we were headed when we turned off the main highway onto a small hinky-dinky winding road. At least Paul knew where we were going. Not too much farther along, we came to the house with the stove.

Paul put money down as a deposit and told the gentleman to hold the stove until we came back. When we returned, we loaded it onto Paul's truck and then he paid the man the rest of the money and Paul dropped me off back at my office so I could get back to "work."

I was eventually promoted to Assistant Vice President, and the next year I was promoted to Vice President.

While we enjoyed our time on the farm, Kathy and I made the decision to sell. We bought a ranch-style house on five acres which was mostly wooded. Before we moved, we had the hardwood floors sanded, the whole house painted, and replaced the air conditioner.

During this transition, Kathy was on a project in Puerto Rico and was unable to get home. I had to handle the entire move. She had not even seen the inside of the new house. In fact, we had to draw up a Power of Attorney so I could purchase the house on our behalf.

Shortly after the move, Kathy's company paid my airfare so I could go to Puerto Rico to see her. The first day I arrived, I was on my own. I went down to the lobby to see if I could tour the city by bus. The man at the desk told me there was such a bus, but the service did not start for another hour. He suggested that I get into a poker game the hotel was hosting. He said I could win one hundred dollars and it was free to enter. I thought, *What do I have to lose?*

While I was playing cards, a lady named Ms. Alivia sat down beside me. We started talking and she asked what I did for a living. I told her I was a bank vice president in the United States, and she said she was a retired school librarian.

I asked her about the city bus route. We both played cards and just talked until someone else won the game. Ms. Alivia explained that the hotel hosted the card game to try to keep folks at the hotel. Once the casino opened up for the day, it was otherwise expected you would go in and play.

Well, Ms. Alivia and I went to the casino and she was a big winner that day! I couldn't believe it when she asked if I would go with her downtown to the courthouse to cash in her $10,000. She also asked if I would help her decide how to invest her winnings.

I agreed and we both got back on the bus headed toward the bank. She confessed she had lost $15,000 at the same casino two nights earlier. She knew she wanted to invest her winnings somehow so she could not readily get to the money. She asked for my help with an overall investment strategy.

The more she talked, I could tell she knew the bank's investment officers. At the bank, she introduced me as a friend and Vice President of a United States bank. She defined my role as her advisor. She decided to invest in Certificates of Deposit and my advice to her was to tier her CDs.

We took the bus to a little sandwich shop where the food was delicious and cheap, then hopped back on the bus to the hotel, where Ms. Alivia went on her own way.

When Kathy's work day was over, she and I went to a seafood restaurant that served baked fish encased in salt. I thought it would taste salty, but it was actually delicious. I told Kathy what happened with Ms. Alivia. She said it sounded just like something I would do, and she was right.

After dinner, Kathy and I went back to our hotel where they had a mini casino. We were both surprised to see Ms. Alivia playing the slot machines. We surmised that she must be a compulsive gambler.

BANK SHENANIGANS

In those days, there were many companies that had phone numbers with an area code of "888." This was a toll call that usually charged by the minute. You could dial an 888 number and listen to a woman explain her sexual experiences. Of course, her job was to keep you on the line as long as possible, so you would be charged an extravagant amount of money.

Somehow Paul Peak, the bank president, found out several 888 calls had been made from inside our bank. Of course, it became my job to find out who was placing these calls.

When I dialed the 888 number that was listed on our phone bill, and explained the reason for my call, the woman did not want to give out what she explained was "privileged information." So I explained that I could easily get a subpoena. She reluctantly gave me the extension the calls had been placed from, but not the person's name.

Thank goodness everyone at our bank had an assigned extension. I was able to track the line and inform the president who had made these calls. I asked if he was sure he wanted to know who it was. "I do," he answered. That employee was terminated the same day.

Shortly after arriving at work one morning in August 2003, I heard what sounded like a bomb going off. The whole building shuddered.

I rushed outside and saw that a jet plane had crashed into the house next door. Both the plane and house were in flames. It was obvious that no one could have survived such an accident.

Thank goodness there wasn't anyone hurt in the house, but little did I realize the jet pilot was someone I knew, Robert Martin.

Robert had been out flying his two-seat Aero L-39Zo Albatros, a privately owned military training jet. One of his employees, Audrey Warfield, responded in a newspaper interview that Robert Martin was an exceptional pilot. His plane went down about fifteen minutes after takeoff. Witnesses on site said the craft was flying over the airpark when it pulled up and fish-tailed before taking a nose dive. To say it was a tragic accident would be an understatement.

Another day, Paul called me into his office. He asked me to read a letter he had received, given to him by our cleaning lady who had found it in the dumpster. The letter was written from a woman to a man, filled with sexual inuendo about all she wanted to do to him the next time they got together.

I had seen a lot of things in writing, but after reading this letter out loud, even I blushed.

Once I finished, Paul handed me the phone book and asked me to call the phone number for the man the letter was addressed to. When I called, the lady of the house answered. "Why did you throw your trash in our dumpster?" I asked. She stated she had no idea what I was talking about, but said she could come up to discuss the issue.

Paul said he didn't want to be alone when she arrived so I stayed. When the lady got there, she asked if she could see the letter. The more she read, the redder her face became. "Can I keep this letter?" she asked. "I promise you this will not happen again." Then she slammed the door on her way out.

A couple of months later, Paul handed me the newspaper and pointed to a notice for her divorce. Sure enough, we never saw any more letters.

After that earlier incident, one of our employees noticed someone routinely dumping their trash in our dumpster. They gave me the license plate number for the truck in question. I called a friend at the sheriff's office and asked him to run the tag number. He agreed, but told me if anyone asked where I got the name, I was not to say where it came from. I told him, "You've got a deal."

After about a week, I called my contact and asked if he had found the owner of the truck. He was reluctant to give me the name because the owner's wife worked for the sheriff's department. I promised I wouldn't tell anyone the information had come from him.

The truck belonged to Paul, our bank president! Now how was I going to tell my boss about how I knew it was him? When he asked, I simply said someone was dumping their crab shells in our dumpster. He never brought it up again because he immediately knew that I knew who the real culprit was.

One strange incident seemed to follow another. Someone from the bank was making calls after midnight and I was asked to find out who it was.

When I dialed the number in question and told the gentleman why I was calling, he said he had no idea what I was talking about. He worked night shift so no one should be calling his house after midnight. I asked him to contact me if he found out who it was. He agreed.

About a week later, this man reached out to me. Apparently one of our employees was calling his wife while he was a work!

I apologized for asking him about the calls, but he seemed glad, because otherwise he would not have known his wife was unfaithful.

KIDS, ETC.

Our daughter Chris was in high school in the mid-1980s, and her teachers there didn't seem to care about helping her deal with her hearing issues. In turn she got bullied because she couldn't understand what people were saying.

I finally went to see her principal. I told him I wanted the bullying stopped and he agreed. For the most part it did, except for one girl who just would not let it go. Chris was afraid to retaliate, however, because she thought she would get in trouble.

When she told us about all of this, we said we would stand up for her if she had to put the girl in her place. So one day our firstborn had finally had enough. She grabbed the girl by the scruff of the neck and stuffed her in a locker.

When Chris came home and told us about the incident, we gave her a hug and told her it was about time. Once the principal heard our side of the story, he said he would take care of the matter. We never heard any more about the incident. Needless to say, that girl never bullied Chris again.

In 1985-86, when Chris was a high school senior, she went out for a drive with her friend Becky. At one point coming around a curve, Becky lost control of her car.

The pair went up and over a pretty steep embankment. The car landed on its roof which left Chris hanging upside down with her seatbelt on.

When the fire company arrived, they had to cut the belt to get Chris out. Thank goodness neither of the girls were injured enough to be taken to the hospital.

The first car Chris had of her own was an older four-door Oldsmobile. It was in good shape and everything worked on it. We all named it "the tank."

One day we got a call from the fire company that she had been in another accident, but had not been hurt. As she went up this steep snowy hill, the car slid over against the wrong side of the road.

While she was waiting for the snowplow, another driver slid down the hill into her passenger side door and got lodged against her car.

We actually received more money from the insurance company than we had paid for the car, so Chris bought a brand-new Chevrolet Cavalier.

In 1987, Chris met David McCarty, and they dated for a few years. They had a church wedding in 1992 with all the trimmings. To say Chris was a beautiful bride would be an understatement.

While working full-time at a local hospital she decided to go back to night school to get a certificate in nursing.

When she graduated, she got her LPN license and shortly afterward took a job as a licensed EMT, working weekends with a local company.

It was a hectic time for her, and unfortunately, the marriage also had its share of trouble. It seemed like it took forever for the divorce to be finalized. Chris pretty much lost everything she had worked for. She came back home until she could get her life back in order.

Most parents can relate to getting a phone call in the middle of the night from a hospital telling you your child has been in a serious car accident. It was September 21, 1991, when we received such a scare.

When we heard Nathan talking in the background, we felt a little relieved... until we received another phone call from his friend telling us our nephew and his best friend had been seriously injured in the incident.

I immediately called my brother and asked if he had heard anything about his son. He said he hadn't, but he'd had a premonition that his son had been killed. I tried to reassure him but he insisted he knew.

When we finally reached the hospital, we found out more details.

Nathan's liver had been severed by his fifth rib and the next seventy-two hours were critical as the liver is like a sponge and very difficult to repair.

Dottie West, a famous country music singer, died in a car wreck from the same type of injury.

The surgeon had never seen a human liver grow back together on its own, but he told us he had seen it happen in animals. That is what we all hoped would happen for our child.

When they told us later that Nathan's was the first human incident where they saw this actually happen, we were all ecstatic.

But my brother's premonition did come true. As Nathan's cousin's funeral was approaching, Nathan persuaded the surgeon to allow him to attend, but he had to agree to follow strict guidelines.

While we were getting all the paperwork together, the surgeon called the nurse who had found Nathan laying in the field. She was the one who called lifeline. When she walked into Nathan's room, she fell to her knees, crying with emotion. When she finally got up, she threw her arms around Nathan. She told us she could not believe he was going to be walking out of the hospital as she never expected him to live.

Even though Nathan was just a teen, he followed the surgeon's recommended guidelines. We had to provide 24-hour care for him, which meant we had to hire someone to be with him during the day. We felt fortunate when we found Ginny, a retired nurse, to help out.

School Board

I did not like the direction the local school district was headed. Instead of just complaining about it, I ran for election to the school board in 1989.

In Pennsylvania, school board directors are unpaid elected public officials. Each school district has nine directors, each fulfilling a four-year term.

Being elected to a school board position means a couple of things. First and foremost, you have to be committed. You learn quickly that you only have one vote. To get anything accomplished, you must get the consensus of at least four other board members who concur with the idea. Just one issue can take up to five years to get passed!

I learned the district routinely received money on a one-time basis and was just letting it sit in a money market fund. I recommended the board should hire a reputable investment company to advise them how to safely invest the funds that would be spent throughout the year.

Nothing happened in this matter until finally I was elected Board President in 1994 (after serving as Vice President the year before). At that point we hired a firm who advised us on other cost-saving ideas.

I will never forget what the Superintendent said when it passed. "Well, this exercise only saved the district ten thousand dollars a year."

I thought to myself, *Ten thousand a year over ten years is $100,000 that could be better used for education.* By the following year we had hired a new Superintendent.

Before I was made Board President, I rarely spoke up in public. In fact I never thought I was capable of public speaking. However, being forced into speaking served me well later in my career when I would make monthly progress reports to the

bank's board of directors. I never felt intimidated or uncomfortable about speaking in public again.

One of my favorite moments happened when I was the first school board president to hand all the students their diploma when they crossed the stage at graduation. It was an especially proud moment because that year's graduates included our son Nathan.

RUSSIAN EXCHANGE TEACHER

One of Kennard-Dale's history teachers, Jeff Hershey, was instrumental in the forming of a diplomatic relationship with School No. 52 in St. Petersburg, Russia.

The overall goal was so our students could learn every aspect of another country's values and language which would become useful later in life. The same could be said for the Russian students.

Soon after we began our program, School No. 52 split and became School No. 631—the only English-speaking school in Russia at that time.

While I served as school board Vice President in 1993-94, Kathy and I had the privilege of hosting two Russian teachers, Lilia and Larisa, as part of the exchange. They came over specifically to immerse themselves in the American culture, our school system, and our Christmas festivities.

Kathy and I took the bus to New York City to meet Lilia and Larisa's flight. Our driver said a snow and ice storm warning had been issued for the area. He asked everyone to grab a bite at the Wendy's restaurant inside the airport so we could get loaded ASAP to start for home.

Sure enough, it started to snow and sleet. All I remember about the ride home was one hill with a stop light at the bottom. Our driver slowed down at the top of the hill and told us to hold on because he wasn't stopping at the bottom, even if the light was red! As luck would have it, just when we approached the light it turned green.

Jeff Hershey planned several day trips for the group. One was to Philadelphia to see Independence Hall, the Liberty Bell, Elfreth's Alley, and other Colonial Philadelphia sights. History students and Social Studies teachers from our district accompanied our Russian visitors.

Another time they went to Baltimore's Inner Harbor for a luncheon cruise down to the Key Bridge.

Of course our visitors visited the elementary and middle school classrooms, as well as the high school. They discussed their impressions of our school compared to theirs.

Our Honor Society students accompanied them to New York City to see the usual sights plus a short visit to the United Nations building.

While in New York they went to the Forbes building to view the large collection of Faberge eggs. Tim Forbes, one of Malcolm Forbes's sons, happened to walk by and talked with Jeff and the group. He was fascinated to hear about our small school having a private exchange relationship with a Russian school.

He asked Jeff for all the details and passed along an application for a grant for funding from the famous Margaret Thatcher

Foundation in Washington. With Tim Forbes as a co-sponsor, Jeff thought our school might have a chance.

Sometimes clubs would help defray trip costs, but thanks to winning this grant, our school district received about $24,000 to subsidize other exchanges as well as our own visit to Russia.

Before Lilia and Larisa arrived at our house, Kathy and I cleaned out our closets so the teachers would have room to hang their clothes. They both expressed a desire to go to Kmart (as Walmart did not have a presence in our area yet). Since there was a Salvation Army store next door to Kmart, Kathy and I decided we could drop off our old clothes and take the Russians shopping all in one trip.

As we approached the Salvation Army store, Lilia and Larisa asked if they could go inside with us. We never made it over to Kmart that day because they enjoyed thrift shopping so much we ran out of time. Instead, we promised them we could return to Kmart another day.

For dinner one night, Kathy made lasagna which they had never tasted. The recipe made enough that Kathy was able to pack up leftovers for them to take on day trips.

My sister held our annual Christmas party at her house. Each family brought toys for their children and placed them under the tree when the kids were not looking. Of course among our presents there just happened to be some gifts under the tree from Santa to both of our Russian teachers.

My brother-in law, my sister, and my brother Scott played instruments on the occasion and Larisa played piano while we all sang along.

The Farmer Boy's Tale

On January 6, 1994, Jeff Hershey, along with all the Russian teachers and their hosts, attended our regular school board meeting. When Jeff introduced these visitors, everyone stood and applauded. It was a moving experience that evening, having Kathy there as a host along with our two Russian teachers. It was also kind of sad too, because their stay was coming to an end.

Before Lilia and Larisa left, they presented Kathy and I with a silver semaver.

We helped them pack and said our goodbyes before they got on the bus.

We knew it was not the end though, as we made plans to visit with each of them later in the year. It somehow softened the tearful exchange.

OUR TRIP TO RUSSIA

The following June 18, 1994, we were invited to go to Russia and stay with the Russian teachers who had stayed with us. Neither Kathy nor I had ever been out of the United States, so we did not know what to expect.

Our guide was Jeff Hershey, who taught Russian language and history at our school.

Our group of mostly teachers flew overnight on Finnair from JFK Airport to Helsinki, where we landed at 8:50 in the morning.

We had to go through Customs there in Finland, then wait for our next flight which wasn't until 7:40 that evening. They took us to a nearby Holiday Inn where we had five "day rooms" available.

Back on the plane, we had another three-hour flight to Moscow, landing at 10:25 P.M., followed by Customs yet again, and then we were transferred to Hotel Izmailova by bus, where the Olympic athletes had stayed.

That night the mirror on the wall fell off. Not exactly a plush hotel. We definitely did not get enough sleep. The next morning, the breakfast was so bad I could not eat it, so I just drank hot coffee.

On Monday, June 20, they took us to see Red Square in the rain. The towers of the Kremlin and the Lenin Mausoleum were most impressive. We walked to the nearby GUM Department Store, which is their version of a giant shopping mall. There was very little merchandise on the shelves.

When we reached the Cathedral of St. Michael inside the Kremlin, the sun finally came out.

St. Basil's Cathedral has very colorful domes. There's nothing like this in Fawn Grove!

On Tuesday we were given a tour inside the Kremlin where we saw the Palace where the Soviet government takes place, along with three cathedrals and the Bell Tower of Ivan the Great.

After dinner we were treated to a performance of the Moscow Circus on ice.

On Wednesday they took us around on the Moscow Metro, which is a subway system. Each station is individually decorated with paintings, sculptures, mosaics, and even chandeliers. They even nicknamed the subway "The People's Museum."

In the afternoon, we went shopping, then we transferred from our hotel in Moscow to an overnight train to St. Petersburg, which became our home on wheels. It also had guards with machine guns.

They told us once we got into our berths to take our belt and tie our door shut. Of course, this made us all a little nervous so we kind of just went from berth to berth and roamed the train instead of going to sleep until the wee hours of the morning.

Thursday we arrived in St. Petersburg where we were met by our first hosts, Lilia and her husband, at the train station. They took us by car to their flat for the first week. They took us to see the *Nutcracker* ballet and the circus. It seemed like the week just flew by.

We toured the beautiful Palace Square. There was a girl's school built by Empress Elizabeth which had formerly been a nunnery but now served as a museum.

We also saw the Church of the Resurrection of Christ and all posed to have our picture taken in The Hermitage, which is the Winter Palace that has numerous paintings by famous artists.

On another day we traveled to the Bay of Finland which was surrounded by woods and marshlands looking out toward the Baltic Sea.

One evening they took us to see *Swan Lake* at the St. Petersburg State Academic Theatre of Opera and Ballet. The inside of the hall was highly decorated, and there were even box seats for the upper crust guests of honor.

Next, we were off to stay with our second host, but to get there we had to go by the rail system which was packed like sardines, but we finally made it.

Our hosts for the second week were Larisa and her husband Serge, and their teenaged daughter Darina. Darina had studied English at her school. Since neither parent could speak English, she became our interpreter. I still stay in contact with Darina via Facebook and email.

Their family did not have a car of their own, so they borrowed Larisa's parents' car for the week. When we went out on the roads, the police would stop them and demand money. They told us not to say anything because if the police found out they had Americans with them, they would demand an even higher fee. So when we got stopped, neither Kathy nor I said a word.

Another day we went to the woods for a Russian picnic.

During our stay, we visited St. Isaac's Cathedral and Marinisky Palace, and got to tour inside both buildings. We also saw a giant statue of Peter the Great on horseback, called "The Bronze Horseman," and later visited Catherine's Palace where she had her own private lake.

Apparently we also needed more culture, so we got dressed up and went to the ballet once more to see a production called *Corsair* in the same theatre.

They took us to visit their school and to an open-air market where they purchased chicken and bread. This was unlike our markets in the U.S. The chickens were hung up by their feet, unrefrigerated, and the bread was a whole loaf of black bread.

It didn't take Kathy and I long to figure out they were not as well off as we were. Even though Larisa worked as a teacher, her husband could not find work in the construction industry.

We told Darina we wanted to prepare lasagna for dinner and asked if her parents would take us grocery shopping. They took us to a Finnish store where we purchased the lasagna fixings.

I will never forget Larisa saying, "Walter, it is too much money to spend." I just kind of chuckled and told her not to worry as it was only fifteen dollars.

Anyhow Kathy fixed lasagna for dinner that evening.

When it was time to leave, I slipped a $100 bill into Darina's hand before we left because I knew Larisa and Serge would be too proud to take any money.

On our last evening, the school hosted a farewell dinner for us.

At the end of our stay, we flew back to Helsinki, Finland, on Saturday, July 1 at 4:50 P.M. After clearing Customs, they took us to the Intercontinental Hotel for the night.

The next morning after breakfast, we went on a whirlwind tour of the Finnish capital, seeing various government buildings, statues, and the open-air market.

Finally they took us to the airport for our homeward flight to J.F.K. Airport at 4:00 P.M. There's no place like home!

ALASKA VIA LAS VEGAS?

Our Alaskan cruise started off a little different than most. First off, we needed a few thousand more airline miles so we could get to travel for free on what would be our one and only Alaskan cruise.

We booked a cheap flight to Las Vegas. We met up with a family we were already friends with from back home while we were there, and decided to visit a casino during the day and take in a show that night.

When we had seen enough of the slot machines and tables, no one could find the exit. We must have looked for an hour before finally making our escape.

We freshened up at our hotels, then reassembled at the Mirage Resort to see Siegfried and Roy with their famous tiger act.

The next day we flew back home, with plenty of "miles" in the bank for the Alaska cruise.

On Sunday, May 21, 1995, we were welcomed aboard the Holland America S.S. Rotterdam in Vancouver, British Columbia in Canada. We did all the customary things like the lifeboat drill and getting our dinner table assignment and cabin keys.

At 5:45 P.M. we finally set sail. We passed Stanley Park and sailed underneath the Lions Gate Bridge into the Strait of Georgia. This path would take us along the inside passage from Vancouver to Ketchikan, along the British Columbia coastline.

On Monday at approximately 11:00 A.M. we entered Lama Passage and cruised past the village of Bella-Bella, Prince Island and on past Triple Island Lighthouse.

Since we were on a boat, we felt we would take advantage of the time by playing card games and just relaxing in the onboard casino.

We both played blackjack. We happened to be seated next to the parents of MLB Colorado Rockies outfielder Larry Walker. They insisted that I take a picture with them. Kathy was dealt three sevens for "21" and won a bottle of champagne. Of course the other one of us did not win anything.

Around 3:00 A.M. our ship crossed the border between Canada and the U.S.A.

We approached Ketchikan via the Nichols Passage and Tongass Narrows. Our docking procedure commenced around 6:45 A.M. on Tuesday. Neither of us knew what to expect, but Ketchikan was an impressive island with a lively past.

The most famous of its red-light districts are "Black Mary," "Blind Polly," and "Dolly's." These houses of ill repute have since been retired, though. Now they are a quiet collection of coffee shops, boutiques, and galleries.

Ketchikan is known as the Salmon Capital of the world, so we took out a charter boat and went fishing for King salmon. Unfortunately, we both came back disappointed at our lack of catch, but we did see a bear along the shoreline and some bald eagles in their gigantic nests.

The ship set sail for Juneau via the Tongass Narrows and Clarence Strait. Around 7:00 that evening, we sailed through the snowy passage into the Sumner Strait. What a sight to behold!

On Wednesday, May 24, we went around Cape Decision, through the Chatham Strait, Fredrick Sound, and Stephens

Passage on our way to Juneau. We were all welcomed with a celebration of the arts and enjoyed the special events and cultural events planned for their Mayfest.

Juneau is nestled between Mount Juneau and Mount Roberts which is a beautiful setting with natural protection against the cold winds and permafrost, which are so much part of Alaska.

Juneau has been the capital of Alaska since 1906, well before it became a U.S. state in 1959. Apart from the man-made wonders of Juneau, Mendenhall Glacier had one of the most spectacular views in the area. At the time the frozen river of ice was 12 miles long and one and a half miles wide.

We departed Juneau around 5:30 A.M. and entered Gastineau Chanell near Marmion Island, headed for the next port of call, Sitka.

The Northern Pass led us into Cross Sound. We passed Cape Spencer on the starboard side, then Cape Edgecombe before entering Sitka Sound.

Sitka is a very diverse city, rich in history and culture. Formerly the Russian/American capital of the District of Alaska, Sitka welcomed us with festivals specific to its native and Russian heritage.

Back in 1867, U.S. Secretary of State William H. Seward purchased Alaska from Russia for $7.2 million. Known as "Seward's Folly," it became a territory of the United States. This city was previously known as "New Archangel" while under Russian rule, but was renamed Sitka, which is the Tlingit word for "the place." Sitka served as Alaska's first capital until 1906.

That night we were on our way to Hubbard Glacier. We hoped the visibility would be clear enough to view Mount Edgecombe, a volcanic mountain with an elevation of 3,371 feet, but no such luck.

We sailed through the night on a northwesterly course to the Gulf of Alaska, reaching Disenchantment Bay—the most northern point of the Yakutat Bay—around 9:00 A.M. on Friday.

Kathy and I both had to put on heavier coats as we approached Hubbard Glacier, named for Gardner Hubbard, a man who served as regent of the Smithsonian Institute and is best known as the founder of the National Geographic Society. We got lucky to see the ice calving off the glacier—a sight not many get to see. As our Alaskan cruise was winding down, that made a great memory to bring home with us.[2]

---

[2] In both 1986 and 2002, the Hubbard Glacier made national news as it "galloped" across Russell Fjord, effectively sealing off the fjord from the ocean, trapping dolphins, seals, and other sea creatures before eventually breaking and releasing its captives to the sea.

In the early Saturday morning hours, we sailed in the Prince Edward Sound where we docked at Port Valdez. First explored by the Spanish in 1790, it was more than 100 years before the area was utilized as a stepping stone to Yukon goldmines.

On March 27, 1964, an earthquake and tsunami destroyed the town. It took five years to rebuild, but Valdez never regained the allure it had before the earthquake.

We disembarked around 11:30 A.M. and set sail on an excursion to the Columbia Glacier. It was not as spectacular as the Hubbard Glacier and we did not spend a lot of time there but it was nice to see.

From Valdez, our ship sailed through the Wells Passage to College Fjord, then down the Gulf of Alaska toward the entrance to Resurrection Bay, heading to our final port, Seward.

The ship docked early Sunday morning at Seward. We had a great time on our first cruise, witnessing all the creatures in their natural environment.

Australia Bound

Once Kathy retired, she discovered she had accumulated enough Marriott points to take the entire family on a trip to Australia at very little out-of-pocket expense.

We decided to ask the children if they would be interested in going along as we felt this would probably be the last trip we would make as a family unit.

Nathan spoke up first and said he would go. Christina and her husband David both said they would go, too. Then at the last minute, David backed out.

We spent the night on Tuesday, May 19, 1998, at a hotel near Dulles Airport in Washington, D.C., since our flight would be leaving at 7:30 the next morning and we would need to be at the airport by 5:30 A.M. The first segment took us to San Francisco where we landed at 9:58 A.M. Pacific time. Since the long flight to Australia didn't leave until 11:00 P.M., we rented a car and got to see a bit of California first, including the Golden Gate Bridge.

After arriving Friday, May 22, 1989, in Sydney, Kathy had booked two "day rooms" for us at the Sheraton Airport Hotel, then we got on Rail Australia Service for the overnight trip to Brisbane. The train departed at 4:24 P.M. and arrived the next morning at 6:00 A.M. where we picked up our rental car and got checked in at the Marriott Surfers Paradise Resort Hotel where we would stay for the week. We joked that even the fish lived in Paradise there.

On Monday, we toured the famous Currumbin Wildlife Sanctuary which is a zoological garden in Queensland, Australia. It was built in 1947 and continues to be added to. They had almost every exotic animal for which Australia is noted, including emu and kangaroos.

We had great fun with the wild lorikeets. The guide gave us a tin plate full of birdseed, and the birds landed all over our heads and arms to eat.

Of course, they had adorable koala bears. They only allowed one person per party to hold and pet one. Chris wouldn't do it because she said it would stress them out, but we did pet some of their kangaroos. One mother had a baby in her pouch. When she bent over, it looked like she had six legs.

We were thankful for the opportunity to see so many of Australia's native animals that we don't have in the United States.

On Tuesday, we drove to see an aboriginal village where we had a meal and watched a native dance performance of the corroboree.

It was fascinating seeing the local people perform their signature dance. They even enticed Chris to get up and dance with them. They were kind to us even though we were outsiders to their country, and treated us and their other guests like royalty. We all had a great day.

The next morning we took a tour of the O'Reilly's treetop walk, where we saw all kinds of birds and a lone koala bear in the wild. It wasn't such a high climb and the sights were remarkable.

On Thursday, Kathy and I went on a bus tour while Chris and Nathan stayed at the hotel and just relaxed. We returned early and I took a nap. By that point we were all pretty worn out. Heading home the next evening would make for a hard day of travel.

On Friday, we returned in our rental car and departed Brisbane on Rail Australia Service at 7:00 P.M. We were all sorry to leave. The people had been so nice and our accommodations were top notch. Even Nathan wanted to stay.

The train arrived in Sydney the next morning and we caught a taxi to O'Malley's where we stayed overnight at the hotel at 228 William Street, Kings Cross 2011.

Kathy and I went to visit Sue Thompson Marsh and her husband Joe. We met up at a restaurant and had a great time talking about home and of course Australia. Kathy's mother had been a babysitter to Sue and her siblings when she was little. When Sue graduated from high school, she got a job teaching English in Australia. While there she met Joe and married him. She never returned to the U.S. except for visits. "I have no reason to go back. I've fallen in love with my life the way it is."

We almost did not allow enough time to get to the airport on Sunday morning. When we told the taxi driver our flight time, he was unhappy with us. "Hold on!" he said. We got there on time, but what a ride!

Nathan was sitting in the front seat. When the driver went through a red light and up onto the sidewalk, Nathan got white as a sheet and grabbed the dashboard. Chris grabbed the back of the seat and held on for dear life. We all felt we were not going to make it to the airport... but we did.

We laughed about it on the plane ride home. "I thought American taxi drivers were crazy," said Kathy, but we never wanted another ride like that one.

We left the Sydney airport at 1:00 P.M. after going through Customs and with the time change, arrived in San Francisco at 9:20 A.M. But the journey was not nearly over. Our next flight departed for Dulles Airport in Washington, D.C., at 12:20 P.M. and did not land until 8:24 P.M., East Coast time.

All in all, it was 20 hours of travel. We were sad our great adventure was over, but I think we were also all glad to be home.

Y2K Scare

As the year 2000 approached, everyone feared what would happen when computers needed to roll from 1999 to 2000. Was the "Y2K" scare a hoax? Or was it real? It really didn't matter for us. Since Forest Hill State Bank was a member of the FDIC, we were required to follow their guidelines at our institution.

I was put in charge of the project, and had to make sure the bank would not have any issues that would reflect negatively on their ability to operate properly on January 1, 2000.

The first thing I did was to create a spreadsheet of the FDIC guidelines alongside our expected timeline to meet them. This made it much clearer to explain at monthly Board of Directors meetings.

To make a long story short, everything worked as planned when the bank opened on January 1, 2000… and I was given a handsome bonus for my efforts.

In 2003, Kathy finally earned her Bachelor of Science degree in Business Management and Communications from the University of Maryland. It was a long haul. I tried to support her decision to go back and get her degree.

Panama Canal
Our Last Adventure

Our next vacation was a cruise to the Panama Canal in February 2010. Three couples decided to do the trip together. Henry and his wife Glenda Jean Sommers offered to take us with them on the way down and back to BWI Airport. We paid half of the fees to park his vehicle in the covered garage. The drive there went perfectly and we parked in a designated spot, with no idea that getting back home later would be a different kind of trip entirely.

We set sail Monday, February 1 on the Zuderdam, which is owned by Holland America. By the time we got settled in our cabins then explored the cruise liner, it was time for the evening meal. We all decided to get a good night's sleep and meet in the morning.

The six of us ate breakfast and lunch together, then played a couple hands of cards and set a time for dinner.

That evening, someone came up with the bright idea to try a sample of every dessert on the menu. By the time the meal was over, we were stuffed.

On Wednesday, Kathy and I went to the onboard art auction. To entice bidders, they gave everyone a free raffle entry into a drawing to win a piece of art. Wouldn't you know, Kathy won one of the prizes! I think getting there early helped her chances. We mailed the Tolkien lithograph back to Pennsylvania in a tube, then had it professionally mounted after we returned. It still hangs in our home today.

On Thursday, we docked in Oranjestad, Aruba at 8:00 A.M. Kathy and I took a half-day tour, visiting the Bushiribana goldmine ruins, the Casibaria rock formations, the California Lighthouse, and the Aloe Vera Factory. When we returned, the natives performed a local dance and we had one of the best meals they had to offer.

What a wonderful way to experience the beauty of Aruba. Back onboard, we freshened up and met our travel companions for dinner.

The next day was spent sailing for the island of Curacao. We arrived on Saturday morning. By the time we all decided what tour we wanted to take, there weren't many options left. So four of us took the Cloud Forest walking tour. We hiked along beautiful trails. As we walked, we came upon an open hummingbird garden. Not only were the tiny creatures beautiful, but they also performed spectacular aerobatic maneuvers.

After this great experience we headed to the first of four suspension bridges that collectively cover a half-mile of mid-air trail—and give a bird's eye view of the cloud forest. These bridges were suspended up to 126 feet above the ground, but it just did not seem like we were up that high.

As we continued hiking, we came across several species of birds, butterflies, and small mammals. We saw heliconias, ferns, orchards, and bromeliads, which were part of this intriguing island's habitat.

Again, we all dined together and enjoyed the rest of the sailing to arrive at the Panama Canal on Monday, February 8. The famed canal connects the Atlantic and Pacific Oceans through a narrow isthmus. It is one of two of the most strategic artificial waterways in the world, allowing ships sailing between the U.S. east and west coasts to avoid needing to sail all the way around Cape Horn, South America—shortening the voyage by about 3,500 miles!

The canal officially opened in August 1914, owned and administered by the Republic of Panama. It is a series of three locks that cost more than $350 million to build. During the construction from 1904 through 1913, more than 56,000 workers were employed. Unfortunately, some 5,600 were killed.

The fatalities may be even higher though, since only deaths that occurred in hospitals were recorded.

The ship arrived in this area at 6:00 A.M. and a couple of us camped out along the rail to save spots so the others could get a bird's eye view of our great big ship passing through those narrow locks.

It was just breathtaking to witness in real time. Words alone cannot describe what we saw. Kathy took a special interest in the area because when her father was in the Army during World War II he had been stationed there.

Several members of our group took the tour of the Banana Plantation while the rest of us just toured the local village and took in the sights. Apparently some local women do not wear tops, so they were bare-breasted. There were booths selling local wares, but we just looked around. I bought and mailed a postcard back home for Kathy to receive later.

The plantation tour explained the entire process of harvesting bananas and getting them ready to ship around the world, as many ships pass through the Panama Canal locks.

That night we set sail for Costa Rica and arrived midday on Tuesday. Kathy and I toured the Rainforest Skywalk. We really enjoyed Costa Rica's enchanting Pacifica rainforest from the air and the water from Puntarenas. We even walked through treetops on a series of hanging bridges at a private reserve.

Then we cruised down the Tarcoles River, home of the famous crocodiles. In between, we enjoyed time shopping and a snack at a quaint Spanish colonial settlement.

We returned in time to freshen up and meet the rest of the crew for dinner. Little did we know that back home folks were facing the beginning of a two-day blizzard, February 9-10.

Our ship sailed all day and night Wednesday, February 10, and we enjoyed the warm weather while others suffered the Mid-Atlantic's worst snowstorm in a long time—10 to 20 inches of snow! The storm began as a classic "Alberta Clipper" in Canada, moving southeast, and finally curving northeast while rapidly intensifying off the New Jersey coast, forming an eye. News media likened it to a Category 1 hurricane, giving it the nickname "Snoverkill."

On Thursday we continued sailing toward Ft. Lauderdale, Florida, and started hearing stories about what we were about to face when we got home. Somehow it was hard to imagine a blizzard while still having such good weather on board the ship.

Nathan called while we were still aboard the cruise liner. He told us they were experiencing one of the worst snowstorms in recent history. He wasn't positive we could even make the flight back to BWI. Kathy and I kind of shook it off, but we could tell the sea was getting rougher as the night progressed. In fact, some of our party got seasick and others could not finish their meal.

After we disembarked, we found out our 11:00 A.M. flight back to BWI had been delayed until later that evening because it was snowing. Not knowing what to expect, we all decided to take a hovercraft ride around one of the many swamp areas in Florida. As none of us had packed a jacket, we were all cold and glad when the ride was over.

After returning to the airport, we finally flew back to BWI. Getting the rest of the way turned out to be a different story though.

We made it to within about ten miles of home when we came upon a patch of highway that looked too deep even with Henry's four-wheel drive. The vehicle got stuck in the snowdrift, but he was able to back out of it. Then he asked us to get out and push. Of course, none of us were dressed for the occasion, but we all got out and started to push the car forward.

As Henry made his way out of the drift, his wife Glenda Jean fell face down into the snow. Kathy and Glenda remarked it was a good thing Henry had not had to back up, or he could have run her over. Henry and I both chuckled.

By the time we reached their home it was already late, so they invited me and Kathy to stay at their place overnight. After breakfast they took us home to a driveway full of snow. This was an exceptional vacation and seeing the locks of the Panama Canal had been a lifelong dream come true. With the Coronavirus pandemic, and everything going on in the world today, perhaps this will be our last cruise.

End of an Era

In 2001, I elected to step down as School Board President, though I remained a board member during the construction of the new Kennard-Dale High where a plaque in the hallway commemorates the dedication and includes my name along with the other school board members.

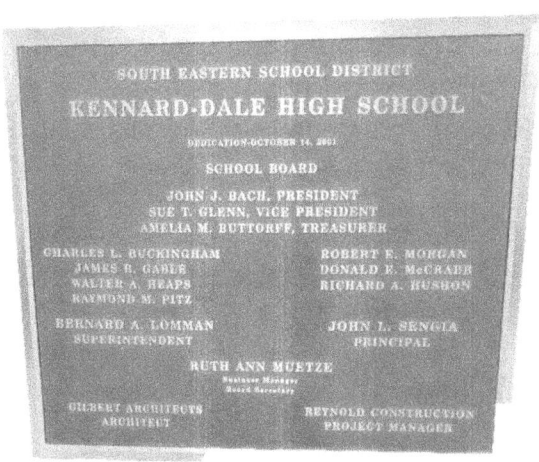

Our daughter Chris has remarried and has a good paying job. Kathy and I could not be prouder of how she has turned out.

They say parents should never play favorites and we have tried to treat both of our children the same.

Nathan is a healthy young man. We are also extremely proud of him and know he can manage on his own. But as parents we still interfere periodically.

He has two healthy sons and a step-daughter and step-son. Nathan is living proof that miracles still happen and that is why we call him our miracle son even today.

When the Forest Hill State Bank that I knew so well was sold in early 2005, and all my superiors had to leave, I felt it was time for me to think about retiring.

After consulting with Kathy, I made the ultimate decision and retired from Mercantile County Bank as Vice President in September 2005. I wanted to leave without any ceremony, but the powers that be decided they wanted to hold a retirement party. They invited Kathy, Chris, Nathan and his wife at the time, and I brought my brothers along.

The decision was not easy, but I'm glad I retired when I did. I got to do all the little jobs at home that I had let go while I was working. And I finally made the decision to write about my life and try to tell Harold Dinsmore's story in such a way that he would be proud and can rest in peace.

About a month after I retired, Paul Peak suffered a massive heart attack on September 11, 2005. I knew then I had made the right decision to retire. I'd already felt the effects of death enough in my lifetime.

After looking back, I have come to the conclusion that you, and maybe your higher power, help create your own luck. It's not going to just come to you.

Acknowledgments

Thanks to:

Kathryn (Kathy) Heaps, my sounding board during this project, and whose detailed family scrapbooks made all of this much easier.

Demi Stevens, whose guidance and support was invaluable.

Whiteford Library in Whiteford, MD, and Kristen, whose interest and insight helped in gathering information.

Kennard-Dale High School Art Class, led by Alex Bastian, and especially Gabrielle (Gabby) Williams, whose expertise made the book cover come to life.

Paul Dinsmore and Susan Bonneville, Harold Dinsmore's brother and sister, who helped fill in the blanks about his home life.